otherTraditions

The Charles Eliot Norton Lectures

John Ashbery

other Traditions

HARVARD UNIVERSITY PRESS

CAMBRIDGE, MASSACHUSETTS

LONDON, ENGLAND · · · 2000

The poems "Unread Pages," "No More Are Lovely Palaces," and "Satur-day Night" (and postamble) by Laura (Riding) Jackson, and the selection on page 101 by Laura (Riding) Jackson from the introduction of *Selected Poems in Five Sets,* copyright © 1991 by the Board of Literary Manage-ment of Laura (Riding) Jackson, are reprinted by permission of Persea Books, Inc. (New York). "In conformity with the late author's wish, her Board of Literary Management asks us to record that, in 1941, Laura (Riding) Jackson renounced, on grounds of linguistic principle, the writing of poetry: she had come to hold that 'poetry obstructs general attainment to something better in our linguistic way-of-life than we have.'" The two poems from "Sonnets in Memory of Samuel," nos. I and IV, from *The Close Chaplet* by Laura Riding Gottschalk are reprinted by permission of the Laura (Riding) Jackson Board of Literary Management.

The poems "Why Must You Know?" "Any Friend to Any Friend," "North Atlantic Passage," and "Train Ride" by John Wheelwright, from *Collected Poems of John Wheelwright,* copyright © 1971 by Louise Wheelwright Damon, are reprinted by permission of New Directions Publishing Corp.

The poems "Monterey," "Kind Valentine," "Midston House," "The Visi-tor," "The Mark," "Peter and Mother," and "The Happy Traveler" by David Schubert are reprinted by permission of The Quarterly Review of Literature.

LIBRARY OF CONGRESS CATALOG CARD NUMBER 00-039648

CIP DATA AVAILABLE FROM THE LIBRARY OF CONGRESS

ISBN 0-674-00315-2

Preface

As the millennium drew near, I became increasingly aware of not having fulfilled the bargain made ten years previously when I accepted the Norton lectureship, that of preparing the lectures for publication. My usual tendency to procrastinate was reinforced by the quantity of practical questions involved: concocting footnotes, checking facts, correcting errors, and a host of other problems that a poet is only too happy to postpone in the hope of frittering away the time writing poems. The main problem was that of transforming a lecture into an essay, the spoken language and the written one being subtly at odds with one another. It may have been harder for me since the spoken language is the one I use when I write poetry. Luckily I have a friend who is a superb poet as well as a former book editor and now a professor of literature at the United States Merchant Marine Academy, where she runs a tight ship. Rosanne Wasserman also possesses all the computer skills without which it seems impossible to get anything done these days, and which I was apparently born too early to master. She has been of immense help to me, typing and editing my manuscript and tracking down elusive references, as has her husband Eugene Richie, also a poet and professor. Eugene's practical assistance sometimes extended to driving me to Cambridge to give a lecture while I was putting finishing touches to it in the back seat. I am enormously indebted to both of them, as well as to my friend David Kermani for his intangible but indispensable moral support. More of the same was supplied by hospitable friends in Cambridge, Ed Barrett and his wife Jenny. (Ed teaches poetry at MIT, an even more unlikely incubator for it than the Merchant Marine Academy.) And still more was laid on by the poet Bill Corbett and his wife Beverly at their comforting house in Boston's South End. Helen Vendler and Seamus Heaney were kind presences at Harvard, offering much-appreciated encouragement, as did the late Harry Levin, whom I had the good fortune to study under when an undergraduate. Theodore and Renée Weiss of Princeton most helpfully put me in touch with David Schubert's widow, Judith Kranes (now deceased), and allowed me to reprint a letter that William Carlos Williams had written them concerning Schubert. Stratis Haviaras kindly put the resources of the Lamont Poetry Room at my disposal. Henri Zerner, the art historian who knows about everything, buoyed me by confiding that his friend Charles Rosen hadn't turned in his Norton lectures yet. (They have since been published.) Finally, I would like to thank my editors at Harvard University Press for their soothingly professional editorial know-how.

Contents

⌃ John Clare

"Grey Openings Where the Light Looks Through"

When I found myself holding the Charles Eliot Norton chair, my thoughts turned to wondering why I had been chosen for this honor. I was somewhat in the dark about this, since the anonymous committee who announced the choice gave no hint of what they expected of me. Naturally, I did have a few theories, however. The first one that came to mind was that, since I am known as a writer of hermetic poetry, in the course of lecturing I might "spill the beans," so to speak: that is, I might inadvertently or not let slip the key to my poetry, resolving this vexed question once and for all. There seems to be a feeling in the academic world that there's something interesting about my poetry, though little agreement as to its ultimate worth and considerable confusion about what, if anything, it means.

Unfortunately, I'm not very good at "explaining" my work. I once tried to do this in a question-and-answer period with some students of my friend Richard Howard, after which he told me: "They wanted the key to your poetry, but you presented them with a new set of locks." That sums up for me my feelings on the subject of "unlocking" my poetry. I'm unable to do so because I feel that my poetry is the explanation. The explanation of what? Of my thought, whatever that is. As I see it, my thought is both poetry and the attempt to explain that poetry; the two cannot be disentangled. I know this isn't going to satisfy anybody and will probably be taken as another form of arrogance from an off-putting poet. On occasions when I have tried to discuss the meanings of my poems, I have found that I was inventing plausible-sounding ones which I knew to be untrue. That does seem to me to be something like arrogance. In any case, as a poet who cares very much about having an audience, I'm sorry about the confusion I have involuntarily helped to cause; in the words of W. H. Auden, "If I could tell you, I would let you know."[1] I'm also mildly distressed at not being able to give a satisfactory account of my work because in certain moods this inability seems like a limit to my powers of invention. After all, if I can invent poetry, why can't I invent the meaning? But I'll leave it at "mildly distressed." If I'm not more apprehensive, it's probably because of a deep-seated notion that things are meant to be this way. For me, poetry has its beginning and ending outside thought. Thought is certainly involved in the process; indeed, there are times when my work seems to me to be merely a recording of my thought processes without regard to what they are thinking about. If this is true, then I would also like to acknowledge my intention of somehow turning these processes into poetic objects, a position perhaps kin to Dr. Williams's "No ideas but in things," with the caveat that, for me, ideas are also things. Here I shall fall back on my habit of quoting other writers (disregarding another quotation, Ralph Waldo Emerson's "I hate quotations. Tell me what you know")[2] by quoting George Moore, a writer considerably to the right (or left) of me as regards the presence of ideas in poetry: "Time cannot wither nor custom stale poetry unsicklied o'er with the pale cast of thought."[3] He wrote this in the introduction to a slim anthology of "pure" poetry he edited; by "pure," he meant a poetry totally devoid of ideas. A little further on, he anticipates Williams, a poet he probably wouldn't have cared much for, when he says, "So perhaps the time has come for somebody to ask if there is not more poetry in things than in ideas, and more pleasure in Gautier's *Tulipe* than in Wordsworth's ecclesiastical, political, and admonitory sonnets." The Théophile Gautier poem was a sonnet whose "avoidance of moral questions . . . lifts *La Tulipe* to a higher plane than Keats's sonnet to Autumn." Moore's friend John Freeman protested, "If you can endure no poetry except a description of the external world, your reading will be confined practically to Shakespeare's songs." And the anthology does contain a number of these, as well as two poems by John Clare, whom I will be discussing in this first chapter. (The anthology also virtually excludes John Keats, of whom Moore said, "I think of him too frequently as a pussy cat on a sunny lawn.")[4]

A second possibility occurred to me when I was wondering why I had been invited to give these lectures. But first, let me mention something John Barth said: "You shouldn't pay very much attention to anything writers say. They don't know why they do what they do. They're like good tennis players or good painters, who are often full of nonsense, pompous and embarrassing, or merely mistaken, when they open their mouths."[5] I supposed that since I am known to be a poet and not a scholar, indeed since I am known not to be a scholar, someone thought it might be interesting to have me talk about poetry from an artisan's point of view. How does it happen that I write poetry? What are the impetuses behind it? In particular, what is the poetry that I notice when I write, that is behind my own poetry? Perhaps somebody wondered this. In the end, I decided that this possibility was the one more likely to fulfill expectations. I'm therefore going to talk about some poets who have probably influenced me (but the whole question of influence appears very vexed to the poet looking through the wrong end of his telescope, though not to critics, who use this instrument the way it was intended—I don't think I'll go into that topic now, though it may well creep in later). My list contains only certifiably minor poets. The reasons for this are threefold: first, I doubt I could add anything of value to the critical literature concerning the certifiably major poets whom I feel as influences: W. H. Auden, chronologically the first and therefore the most important influence, as well as Wallace Stevens, Marianne Moore, Gertrude Stein, Elizabeth Bishop, William Carlos Williams at times, Boris Pasternak, and Osip Mandelstam. It will be noted that a number of major twentieth-century poets don't figure in this list, but one can't choose one's influences, they choose you, even though this can result in one's list's looking embarrassingly lopsided. My list of minor poets who have mattered to me would be much longer. Most poets, I suspect, have their own ideas on what the canon ought to be, and it bears little resemblance to the average anthologist's. That is why I at first decided to call this series "The Other Tradition," which I later regretted having done, deciding that it was more accurate to call it "Other Traditions." (Though since every poet has other traditions, perhaps it would be correct after all to refer to these collectively as "The Other Tradition.") Poets who have meant a lot to me at various times are F. T. Prince, William Empson, the painfully neglected English poet Nicholas Moore, Delmore Schwartz (once thought a major poet), Ruth Herschberger, Joan Murray, Jean Garrigue, Paul Goodman, Samuel Greenberg: I could go on, but you get the idea. These are not poets of the center stage, though they have been central for me. If that means I too am off-center, so be it: I am only telling it as it happened, not as it should have happened.

In addition to the poets one has at times been influenced by, there is also a much smaller group whom one reads habitually in order to get started; a poetic jump-start for times when the batteries have run down. For me, the most efficacious of these has always been Friedrich Hölderlin, but since I can't read him in the original and since he is in any case a major poet, I wouldn't dream of discussing him. Pasternak (especially in the little-known translation of J. M. Cohen, which I discovered many years ago in the Lamont Poetry Room) and Mandelstam are two other major writers I use for this purpose. Among the minors, with one exception I have chosen to talk in this series about the jump-start variety, poets I have at some period turned to when I really needed to be reminded yet again of what poetry is. They are John Clare, Thomas Lovell Beddoes, John Wheelwright, Laura Riding, and David Schubert. The exception is the French writer Raymond Roussel, for whom I feel enormous empathy, though I can't say that reading him ever directly inspired me to write. The influence came in a curiously backward and indirect way, so that I was only conscious of it much later, and am still discovering traces of it I hadn't realized were there.

These constitute a very mixed bag of writers, though good things sometimes come in mixed bags. I may have presumed too much in selecting a group whose only link is that they have at times been very important to my development as a writer. For those to whom this is a matter of indifference, I can only hope that the relative unfamiliarity of most of them and the fact that most haven't received enormous attention from critics will be a sufficient reason for reading this book.

As I look back on the writers I have learned from, it seems that the majority, for reasons I am not quite sure of, are what the world calls minor ones. Is it inherent sympathy for the underdog, which one so often feels oneself to be when one embarks on the risky business of writing? Is it desire for one-upmanship, the urge to parade one's esoteric discoveries before others? Or is there something inherently stimulating in the poetry called "minor," something it can do for us when major poetry can merely wring its hands? And what exactly is minor poetry?

This question is an invitation to frivolity, and Auden did very well in succumbing to it when he wrote the introduction to his anthology, *Nineteenth-Century British Minor Poets*. To the question, "Who is a major, who is a minor poet?" he replies, "One is sometimes tempted to think it nothing but a matter of academic fashion: a poet is major if, in the curriculum of the average college English department, there is a course devoted solely to the study of his work, and a minor if there is not." He continues:

One cannot say that a major poet writes better poems than a minor; on the contrary, the chances are that, in the course of his lifetime, the major poet will write more bad poems than the minor. Nor, equally obviously, is it a matter of the pleasure the poet gives an individual reader: I cannot enjoy one poem by Shelley and am delighted by every line of William Barnes, but I know perfectly well that Shelley is a major poet, and Barnes a minor one. To qualify as major, a poet, it seems to me, must satisfy about three and a half of the following conditions.

   1. He must write a lot.
   2. His poems must show a wide range of subject matter and treatment.
   3. He must exhibit an unmistakable originality of vision and style.
   4. In the case of all poets, we distinguish between their juvenilia and their mature work but, in the case of the major poet, the process of maturing continues until he dies so that, if confronted by two poems of his of equal merit but written at different times, the reader can immediately say which was written first. In the case of a minor poet, on the other hand, however excellent the two poems may be, the reader cannot settle the chronology on the basis of the poems themselves.

He adds, "To satisfy all the conditions is not, as I said, essential. Wordsworth, for example, cannot be called a master of technique, nor could one say that Swinburne's poetry is remarkable for its range of subject matter. Borderline cases there must necessarily be."[6]

One poet who flunks all but one of Auden's tests of a major poet, and who is included in his anthology, is John Clare. It seems to me that Clare escapes Auden's last category. This could be debated. In general, though, there are significant differences between his early and later poems, in part as a result of the madness that kept him in an asylum for most of the last twenty-seven years of his life. Broadly speaking, the early work catalogues, to the exclusion of almost everything else, his rural surroundings near Helpstone, a village in the Northamptonshire fen district, while the later work is more introspective and relatively unadorned, with fewer of those teeming lists of rural ephemera. The early period culminates in the beautiful long poem "The Village Minstrel," probably Clare's most sustained performance, and in a constellation of shorter poems, especially sonnets of a kind unique to him, that became ideal vehicles for the brief, crystal-clear encapsulations of nature at which he excelled. These are rare instances of perfection in a poet whose habit, one might even say whose strength, was imperfection. Many were collected in his first volume, *Poems Descriptive of Rural Life and Scenery*, in 1820. This book was Clare's first and only real success; by the following year, it had gone through four editions, eventually selling more than thirty-five hundred copies, while the publisher, John Taylor, was still trying to unload the five hundred copies of Keats's third volume which he had also printed in 1820.

The "peasant poet" became an overnight success. Taylor invited him to London (the first of four such trips), where he hobnobbed in his green suit with the likes of Charles Lamb, William Hazlitt, S. T. Coleridge, and Thomas De Quincey.

He was introduced to rich patrons who talked of starting a subscription to rescue Clare from day labor. This eventually happened, though the annuity never really covered his needs, and in the end chronic poverty became an aggravating factor in his madness. Then too, the patrons, notably a certain Lord Radstock, began to meddle in his poems, trying to excise Clare's so-called radical sentiments (protests against the evils of enclosure and the plight of the rural poor), anticlericalism, and passages considered sexual or scatological. Clare did, however, form lasting relationships with some of his literary acquaintances, who responded to his poetry and could see through what Clare called his "clownish ways" to the keen intelligence underneath. He jotted down portraits of some of them that are as oddly incisive as his sketches of field mice and burdocks; of Hazlitt, he wrote: "When he enters a room he comes stooping with his eyes in his hand as it were throwing under-gazes round at every corner as if he smelt a dun or thief ready to seize him by the collar and demand his money or his life he is a middle-sized dark-looking man and his face is deeply lined with a satirical character his eyes are bright but they are rather buried under his brows he is a walking satire."[7]

Clare's next book, *The Village Minstrel and Other Poems,* appeared with Taylor in 1821 and was moderately successful, but thanks largely to the publisher's dilatoriness, his third volume, *The Shepherd's Calendar,* didn't appear until 1827, by which time the vogue for Clare and for poetry in general had waned considerably. Taylor's enthusiasm seemed to have waned, too. As editor he had from the first the task of transcribing Clare's rough and unpunctuated manuscripts into something that could be printed, in the process frequently changing the text to eliminate the dialect words and "improprieties" that are so vital an element of the poetry, while generally respecting its substance. But *The Shepherd's Calendar* brought out a new strain of impatience in him, and the published version was senselessly mutilated in a way that the earlier volumes had not been; it is often impossible to second-guess Taylor's reasons for the emendations he made, including wholesale rejection of the July section, for which Clare dutifully supplied an alternate, weaker version. The problem was Clare's limited range, which today everybody recognizes as an element of his poetry, and which his admirers are happy to take in stride. After the first intoxicating novelty of *Poems Descriptive,* which swept through London like a blast of fresh air, readers not unreasonably expected Clare to surprise them anew. But more of the same was precisely the name of his game. From the viewpoint of the late twentieth century, this sameness, for those who value Clare, appears not so much a flaw as the very fabric of his writing. And his formal eccentricities, though unwilled, are less troubling to those who have experienced the poetry of our time. A modern editor of Clare, James Reeves, has put the case nicely: "If one reads Clare's poems in bulk, one can get used to these blemishes, ignore them, or even come to love them, though one may continue to fear that they may put off other readers. For the faults are part of the poems and the poems are the expression of the man . . . His poems are like the central English countryside where they grew, unsensational, undramatic, revealing their beauties more to the dweller than the visitor. The qualities of such scenery are secret and intimate. Yet the poems need selection. The landscape has dull stretches, patches of repetition, and occasional intrusions by non-native elements."[8]

A long poem, therefore, is going to suffer in comparison to a judicious selection of shorter ones. *The Shepherd's Calendar* contains some of Clare's finest writing but it also contains doggerel, and even some of the better stretches are monotonous. It takes a special kind of reader to appreciate it for what it is: a distillation of the natural world with all its beauty and pointlessness, its salient and boring features preserved intact.

Poems from the years up until Clare's first confinement in 1837 do seem to gain in polish, though at bottom their structure remains as idiosyncratic as ever. And the elegiac, valedictory tone that dominates the asylum period begins to thrust itself forward even now. Before his committal to the High Beech asylum at Epping Forest in 1837, there had been a previous upheaval: Clare's removal from Helpstone to the nearby village of Northborough, where he and his family occupied a comfortable cottage provided, not rent-free, by a wealthy patron. This was supposed to be a step up, but though his new home was only three miles from the far more primitive cottage where he had been born and raised, it was a new world for him and a strange one. The sense of loss, linked with an automatic, unreflecting joy in nature, had been the dominant note in his poetry from the beginning. And the losses, as well as the joys, were real. Enclosure arrived at Helpstone in 1809, in Clare's sixteenth year: after that his landscape was never the same, its fens drained, its lovely waste places deforested, ploughed, and fenced off.

Even more devastating was the breaking off of relations with his childhood sweetheart, Mary Joyce, perhaps because of parental objections to Clare's humble status, though some have suggested that she herself was responsible. As time went on, he would, Nerval-like, elevate her to the status of muse and guardian angel, the companion of his dreams, and eventually he grew convinced that she was his wife. ("I sleep with thee, and wake with thee, / And yet thou art not there," he wrote to her from Northampton Asylum in 1842, nine years after her death.)[9] In fact, he had been married since 1820 to Martha Turner, known as Patty, who bore him seven children. They had married on account of Patty's pregnancy, though the marriage seems to have been a fairly happy one; in the asylum, Clare would also write of his two wives, Martha and Mary. Still, the pre-asylum Northborough period saw the creation of some of his most heartbreakingly beautiful sonnets, including "Mouse's Nest" and several fine longer poems, such as "The Flitting" and "Boyhood Pleasures."

Opinion has always been divided on the worth of the asylum poems. At times it has seemed as though the sudden spate of critical studies and editions of Clare's poetry over the past twenty-five years coincided with a new vogue for insanity, due in part to the influential writings of R. D. Laing and Michel Foucault. Perhaps it was in reaction to attitudes like theirs that Donald Davie wrote, with characteristic crustiness: "There will always be sophisticated philistines who prefer, for diagnostic or more dubious reasons, the poems which poets write when out of their wits to the ones they write with their wits about them. Poets nowadays know that it helps their reputations and sales if they can manage a spell in the psychiatric ward. But anyone who goes to poems for poetry and not another thing will prefer the sane Clare of *The Shepherd's Calendar* to the lunatic Clare whose late poetry can be painfully deciphered from pathetic manuscripts."[10] The English poet Elaine Feinstein agrees that "the mad poetry" has won "disproportionate praise."[11] Harold Bloom, however, sees in Clare "a Wordsworthian vision" that attains "a final authority" in some of the asylum poems, and adds that in a few of them "the sense of loss is transformed into a rejection of nature for a humanistic eternity, an apocalypse akin . . . to Blake's."[12] And Mark Storey, perhaps the most diligent modern critic of Clare's poetry, insists that "any balanced and truly sane view of Clare must include an acknowledgment that the asylum poetry represents the culmination and fulfillment of [his] achievement."[13]

There is no doubt that the "trilogy" of poems Bloom singles out for special praise—"An Invite to Eternity," "I Am," and "A Vision"—are the most sublime that Clare wrote and among the greatest poems in English, as anthologists have long recognized. And the notably un-Byronic asylum poem "Child Harold" ranks with *The Village Minstrel* and *The Shepherd's Calendar* as one of his most successful attempts at a long poem, though its somberness and austerity are far removed from those earlier pageants of rustic life. And there are still other treasures, like the Blakean "I Hid My Love" (as far as we can tell, Clare didn't know Blake's poetry) and sometimes a half-comic lapse as in the sonnet "To Wordsworth," where Clare seems momentarily to lose sight of his theme of homage in order to get down in the grass, his favorite occupation, before righting himself: "I love to stoop and look among the weeds, / To find a flower I never knew before; / Wordsworth go on—a greater poet be; / Merit will live, though parties disagree!"[14] And finally there are spar-like fragments of great and enigmatic beauty, such as this late quatrain called "The Elms and the Ashes," for me a talisman-poem: "The elm tree's heavy foliage meets the eye / Propt in dark masses on the evening sky. / The lighter ash but half obstructs the view, / Leaving grey openings where the light looks through."[15]

The fact is that Clare wrote some of his best and worst poetry during his years of confinement. Though he was patently miserable in both institutions, High Beech and Northampton Asylum, they were relatively benign by Victorian standards. He was allowed to ramble outdoors and particularly enjoyed the scenery of Epping Forest, though it was from there that he made his escape in 1841 back to Northborough, a nightmarish journey of which he has left a heartbreaking prose account. Yet a madhouse was a madhouse, and Clare, whose life at the best of times had been riddled with poverty and spiritual anguish, must have passed his long captivity in unrelieved confusion and misery. So it is not very surprising that so much of his poetry falls below his previous standard, albeit in various ways. One example is another painful attempt at a Byronic epic, this time *Don Juan A Poem*. Clare never had much gift for satire, which he tried from time to time in a conscious attempt to broaden his range, notably in "The Parish," a gallery of scathing caricatures of village low-life. Though he here makes a curious effort to achieve the breezy Byronic tone of the master's *Don*

Juan, this work and too many others of his later years are chiefly of clinical interest—though it is hard to dislike totally a poem that contains the lines: "And in a madhouse I can find no mirth pay / —Next Tuesday used to be Lord Byron's birthday" or "Though laurel wreaths my brows did ne'er environ / I think myself as great a bard as Byron."[16]

What is it about Clare that attracts us so much today? I have already alluded to one aspect of him that strikes one almost at the first moment of contact, that is, for want of a more exact term, his seeming modernity. Arthur Symons, who wrote the first valuable twentieth-century essay on Clare, an introduction to a collection of his poems published in 1908, said of him, "He begins anywhere and stops anywhere."[17] Eighty years later, this is not a foible that will raise many hackles: isn't that what poets usually do? Perhaps that is why Robert Graves, more of a modernist than Symons, praised Clare as being "technically admirable" and having "the most unusual faculty of knowing exactly how and when to end a poem."[18] It's hard not to agree with both of them. Yes, Clare often starts up for no reason, like a beetle thrashing around in a weed patch, and stops as suddenly; yes, his sonnets haven't the shapeliness of real sonnets, his longer poems the graceful expansiveness of the odes of William Collins which he so admired, but to our ears they capture the rhythms of nature, its vagaries and messiness, in a way that even Keats never did.

Another side of Clare's modernity is a kind of nakedness of vision that we are accustomed to, at least in America, from the time of Walt Whitman and Emily Dickinson, down to Robert Lowell and Allen Ginsberg. Like these poets, Clare grabs hold of you—no, he doesn't grab hold of you, he is already there, talking to you before you've arrived on the scene, telling you about himself, about the things that are closest and dearest to him, and it would no more occur to him to do otherwise than it would occur to Whitman to stop singing you his song of himself. It is like that "instant intimacy" for which we Americans are so notorious in foreign climes. Clare bears you no ill will and doesn't want to shock or pain you, but that isn't going to make him change his tale one whit; if you suddenly burst into tears, that will seem to him another natural phenomenon, like the rain or the squeal of a badger. He is apt to show you his wounds and crack a joke in the same moment; he is above all an instrument of telling. Nowhere is this more evident and appalling than in the narrative of his escape from High Beech entitled "Journey out of Essex," where he records "going down a very dark road hung over with trees on both sides very thick which seemed to extend a mile or two I then entered a town and some of the chamber windows had candle lights shineing in them," and a few lines later reports matter-of-factly that "I satisfied my hunger by eating the grass by the road side which seemed to taste something like bread I was hungry and eat heartily till I was satisfied and in fact the meal seemed to do me good."[19] The dreamlike vision of the road and the account of his ghastly meal have the same weight for him. What he sees, he is. J. Middleton Murry wrote that "if Wordsworth had seen a primrose as Clare saw it . . . he would have felt that he was seeing 'into the heart of things,' whereas Clare—who seems always to have seen in this way—felt that he was merely seeing things."[20] Like Kierkegaard, Clare could have said of himself: "It seems as though I had not drunk from the cup of wisdom, but had fallen into it."[21]

The sudden, surprising lack of distance between poet and reader is in proportion to the lack of distance between the poet and the poem; he is the shortest distance between poem and reader. We are far from emotion recollected in tranquillity or even the gently shaping music of Keats's grasshopper sonnet. Clare's poems are dispatches from the front. "I found the poems in the fields / and only wrote them down," he wrote, and he tells us that a favorite method of composing was in the open, using his hat as a writing desk.[22] The resulting *plein-air* effect is similar to the studies of John Constable, Clare's exact contemporary. In the case of both, the point is that there is no point. Clare is constantly wandering, in his circumscribed domain, but there is not much to see; the land is flat and fenny and devoid of "prospects." Unlike Wordsworth's exalted rambles in "The Prelude," there is no indication that all this is leading up to something, that the result will be an enriching vision, a placing of man in harmonious relation to his God-created surroundings. Murry says that Wordsworth was engaged in putting the poetry of nature wrong by linking it to a doubtful metaphysic, and John Clare was engaged in putting it right.[23] But the cost of putting things right was enormous, dooming Clare to eternal wandering, with rhyme but without reason, to coming full circle again and again, with the same traveling companions— birds, insects, flowers, occasionally a passing ploughman or a band of gypsies, but essentially alone, mourning the loss of childhood felicity. Much of his work, *The Shepherd's Calendar* in particular, is written in the present tense, a conceit I find annoying in contemporary poetry when the poet is simultaneously having an experience and handing it over to you in the form of a poem. Clare makes this rapid transfer believable, since for him experiencing is the same as telling. Only occasionally does a still point give the measure of this turning world, and then discreetly, as when the activity of January in *The Shepherd's Calendar* is suddenly contrasted with stasis: "While in the fields the lonely plough / Enjoys its frozen sabbath now / and horses too pass time away / In leisure's hungry holiday,"[24] where the irony of "enjoys" leaches through to the surface after one has passed this point in the poem.

My own first experience of Clare was the early poem "Recollections after an Evening Walk." I remember being riveted by the couplet: "The wet bush we past, soon as touch'd it would drop, / And the grass 'neath our feet was as wet as a mop."[25] The almost comical rightness of this image, which at first seems a cliché but isn't (at least I've never heard anyone say "as wet as a mop"—besides, mops aren't always wet, though when they are they would have to resemble the meadow-grass in question), somehow enhanced by the obvious rhyme—Clare was never one to shy away from these, "dog" and "hog" being a favorite—was perfect. One did not feel transported from this squishy scene, but pressed further down into it, until with one's face in the grass one could take in the squillions of dramas in which bugs, worms, and snails were the actors and couch-grass the decor. Another early discovery was this short prose fragment called "House or Window Flies," which started me examining the possibilities of prosaic poetry: "These little indoor dwellers, in cottages and

halls, were always entertaining to me; after dancing in the
window all day from sunrise to sunset they would sip of the
tea, drink of the beer, and eat of the sugar, and be welcome
all the summer long. They look like things of mind or fairies,
and seem pleased or dull as the weather permits. In many
clean cottages and genteel houses, they are allowed every lib-
erty to creep, fly, or do as they like; and seldom or ever do
wrong. In fact they are the small or dwarfish portion of our
own family, and so many fairy familiars that we know and
treat as one of ourselves."[26]

Though the effect of Clare's poetry, on me at least, is al-
ways the same—that of re-inserting me in my present, of re-
establishing "now"—the means he employs are endlessly
varied despite the general air of artlessness. "The Village
Minstrel," for instance, has a narrative glamour that is fes-
tive; the neatly turned epithets and sharp glimpses of village
life fit together like an elaborate piece of clockwork as the
tale of Lubin the minstrel unfolds. Clare stays very close to
depicting the scene at hand until the end, when the village
opens out into a breathtaking panorama:

> Ah, as the traveller from the mountain-top
> Looks down on misty kingdoms spread below,
> And meditates beneath the steepy drop
> What life and lands exist, and rivers flow;
> How fain that hour the anxious soul would know
> Of all his eye beholds—but 'tis in vain:
> So Lubin eager views this world of woe,
> And wishes time her secrets would explain,
> If he may live for joys or sink in 'whelming pain.[27]

Another example of his inspired *bricolage* is the run-on couplets of *The Shepherd's Calendar,* exhausting in the long run but vivid in the sense they give of a self-proliferating world whose accumulation of particulars is finally as convincing as that of "The House that Jack Built," an early favorite of Clare's.

As he sinks deeper into misery, Clare's poetry becomes strangely hushed and pure. In "The Flitting," written before his confinement to High Beech, particulars are smoothed out and the teeming detail of the landscape is absorbed in a classic façade that suggests James Thomson, whom Clare admired more than any other poet, though its urgency is a far cry from Thomson's blandness:

> Time looks on pomp with vengeful mood
> Or killing apathy's disdain;
> So where old marble cities stood
> Poor persecuted weeds remain.
> She feels a love for little things
> That very few can feel beside,
> And still the grass eternal springs
> Where castles stood and grandeur died.[28]

Though the stanzas of "Child Harold," written at High Beech, are given numbers, each seems to begin at the beginning, producing a curious effect of stasis within movement, while the Clarian landscape has begun to be transformed into an emblematic, visionary one reminiscent of the painter Samuel Palmer:

Now harvest smiles, embrowning all the plain
The sun of heaven o'er its ripeness shines
'Peace—plenty' has been sung, nor sung in vain
As all bring forth the maker's grand designs
—Like gold that brightens in some hidden mines
His nature is the wealth that brings increase
To all the world—his sun forever shines
—He hides his face, and troubles they increase
He smiles—the sun looks out in wealth and peace.[29]

Finally, in the handful of perfect lyrics from the last asylum period, all the turbulent details of landscape and loss are distilled in a transparency as seamless and as timeless as the poems of Hölderlin's madness. There is "I Am" with its famous beginning, "I am, yet what I am none cares or knows."[30] There is what Bloom calls "Clare's most perfect poem, the absolutely Blakean 'A Vision'":[31]

I lost the love of heaven above,
I spurned the lust of earth below,
I felt the sweets of fancied love,
And hell itself my only foe.
I lost earth's joys, but felt the glow
Of heaven's flame abound in me.
Till loveliness and I did grow
The bard of immortality.
I loved but woman fell away,
I hid me from her faded fame,
I snatch'd the sun's eternal ray

And wrote till earth was but a name.
In every language upon earth,
On every shore, o'er every sea,
I gave my name immortal birth
And kept my spirit with the free.[32]

Edward Thomas wrote in an essay on Clare: "Words never consent to correspond exactly to any object unless, like scientific terms, they are first killed. Hence the curious life of words in the hands of those who love all life so well that they do not kill even the slender words but let them play on; and such are poets."[33] Clare, who would not hurt a fly or a word, let both play on, but the cost was enormous—nothing less than writing "till earth was but a name." The result for him was long desolation, ending in death. But the rewards for us are great.

⌃ Olives and Anchovies

The Poetry of
Thomas Lovell Beddoes

The life of Thomas Lovell Beddoes bears superficial re-
semblances to that of John Clare. Though Beddoes seems
not to have suffered the poverty that helped to drive Clare
insane, in other respects his career was equally ill-starred.
Both poets, after well-received early publications, more or
less vanished from sight until the twentieth century. Much
of Clare's asylum poetry and almost all of Beddoes's work
survived only because concerned admirers went to the
trouble of copying it out and publishing it. Neither was
favored by accidents of time or geography. Clare, born in
1793, and Beddoes, ten years his junior, arrived on the lit-
erary scene as the sun of Romanticism, hastened by the
early deaths of Keats, Shelley, and Byron, was setting, and
an earlier vogue for poetry was ending. After their youth-
ful successes, both Clare and Beddoes lived far from cen-
ters of literature, Clare in rural Northamptonshire and
Beddoes in provincial Germany and Switzerland, and
both remained more or less out of touch with the writing
of their time. Both worked in outmoded genres ill-
calculated to set the world on fire even if there had been
anybody to notice. And both died tragically: Clare in an
asylum, and Beddoes, who was "much possessed by

death" (as T. S. Eliot said of John Webster),[1] after his second try at suicide, succeeded in a hotel room in Basel. Both led disordered affective lives. During his long confinement, Clare imagined himself married to a woman named Mary who had been dead for years. Beddoes appears to have been homosexual, though evidence for this is scanty, as is most biographical information relating to his adult life. One clue seems to be a line from his most famous (and deservedly so) poem, "Dream-Pedlary," where he speaks of wishing to raise his "loved, longlost boy" from the dead. As for their poetry, Clare and Beddoes are almost diametrically opposed: Clare's is rough and rustic, Beddoes's artificial and willfully decadent, though there are occasions when they seem to overlap. Clare's beautiful but atypical asylum poem, "An Invite to Eternity,"[2] is in the demon-lover mode favored by Beddoes: a lover's invitation to his mistress to accompany him on a harrowing journey to the netherworld.

Beddoes was born at Clifton, Shropshire, in 1803, to a distinguished family. His father, often referred to in his time as the "celebrated Dr. Beddoes," was a colleague of Sir Humphry Davy, who lived with the Beddoes family and taught at the Pneumatic Institution in Clifton, where Dr. Beddoes administered laughing gas to Coleridge (who thought of writing the doctor's biography). According to a contemporary account, these experiments "converted the laboratory into the region of hilarity and relaxation."[3] Wordsworth was another family friend. Beddoes's mother, Anna, was a sister of the novelist Maria Edgeworth, and as a child Thomas sometimes visited her and the other Edgeworth relatives in Ireland. Davy wrote that Anna Beddoes "possessed a fancy almost *poetical* in the highest sense of the word, great warmth of affection, and disinterestedness of feeling, and under favorable circumstances she would have been, even in talents, a rival of Maria."[4]

Dr. Beddoes appears to have been in his own way as eccentric as his son would later become. He too tried his hand at poetry: his long poem entitled "Alexander's Expedition down the Hydaspes and the Indus to the Indian Ocean" has been called "one of the strangest books in English."[5] Beddoes's biographer H. W. Donner tells us that the doctor believed sexual education should begin early: "It was to start with natural history and proceed through the dissection of pregnant frogs and hens to the witnessing of the 'labor pains of a domestic quadruped.'" Donner adds, "There is no telling what sights fed the observant eyes of the little boy who was later to be 'for ever haunted' by the problem and presence of death,"[6] a presence that would draw nearer with the death of Dr. Beddoes when Thomas was six years old and that of his mother when he was twenty-two.

As an undergraduate at Charterhouse School, Beddoes wrote prose narratives of which only "Scaroni" survives, and poetry including a poem on a comet, perhaps the famous one of 1811, which appeared in the *London Morning Post* when the poet was sixteen. He probably also began there his long poem "in three fyttes," "The Improvisatore," which he would publish with other juvenilia as a pamphlet while still a freshman at Oxford. (Beddoes later tried to destroy the press run and was almost successful; only a half dozen copies survive.) These early works promise little for the future except the ghoulish atmosphere which was to be a constant, though there are occasional descriptive flourishes in an "Eve of Saint Agnes" style, such as: "The boughs ice-sheathed shake, bristling out / And coral holly berries pout / in crystal cradles, like the shine / Of goblets flushed with blood-red wine."[7] Besides the comet poem, the pamphlet also contains a suite of thirteen precious "quatorzains," fourteen-line poems similar but not identical to sonnets, and a final poem addressed "To a Bunch of Grapes / Ripening in My Window."

Beddoes's next volume, the only other one published during his lifetime, was "The Bride's Tragedy," which appeared the following year and was an instant success. As was the case with Clare, "It became for a time the town-talk to speak of him," in the words of the biographer John Forster;[8] while the poet George Darley, who hailed Clare as well, called Beddoes "a scion worthy of the stock from which Shakespeare and Marlowe sprung."[9] Beddoes's remaining years at Oxford were restless ones, during which he began and destroyed a number of verse dramas. Of one of these only a single line survives because his friend Thomas Kelsall couldn't forget it: "Like the red outline of beginning Adam."[10] One longs to know more of this work, but even in his surviving and seemingly completed work, Beddoes was to remain "a poet of fragments," as he is often called,[11] and we have no choice but to accept him on these terms.

In 1825, Beddoes left England to study medicine in Göttingen, and thereafter would spend most of the remainder of his life on the Continent. After producing the fragmentary dramas "The Last Man," "Love's Arrow Poisoned,"

"Torrismond," and the substantial hulk "The Second Brother," of which three acts survive, he was to give over the rest of his creative life to the writing and continual revision of his magnum opus, the impossible neo-Jacobean tragedy, "Death's Jest Book." He completed an early version in 1828 and sent it off to friends in England, confident that it would soon be published and hailed as a masterpiece. Unfortunately, his friends—the poet Bryan Walter Procter, who wrote poetry under the pseudonym Barry Cornwall, and the novelist J. G. H. Bourne—counseled him against publishing it without thoroughgoing revisions; and even Kelsall, who favored publication, found its irregularities disconcerting. "Death's Jest Book" was not to appear until 1850, a year after the death of its author, at which time Walter Savage Landor would declare that "nearly two centuries have elapsed since a work of the same wealth of genius as 'Death's Jest Book' was given to the world."[12] But for Beddoes, it became a jinx, siphoning off all his creative energies in futile attempts at revision and completion. Into its infinitely expandable frame went many individual lyric poems of great beauty; when the plot offered no occasion for them, Beddoes would invent one. A band of fishermen is introduced in the first act for no other purpose than to sing a chantey; that accomplished, they disappear forever. The resulting structure was peculiar, to say the least, but Beddoes's friends were wrong in finding it deficient; the bizarrely irregular shape of "Death's Jest Book" is one aspect of its stupefying originality. Though it could be considered a monumental pedestal without a statue, it is still a work that cannot be ignored, that collars the reader, insinuating its poisonous charms, its aroma of rose, sulfur, and sandalwood, into one's nostrils from the very first speech.

Never very confident of his abilities as a writer, Beddoes in his later years turned increasingly to his other passion, medicine, hoping to find the solutions to life's (and death's) mysteries that poetry had refused to yield. He eventually received his M.D. from Göttingen; a renowned doctor there would later call him the best pupil he had had during his fifty years of professorship. Meanwhile, Beddoes claimed to friends that he now preferred "Apollo's pill-box to his lyre."[13] It seemed that he hoped to discover "the exact location of the soul" through anatomical research.[14] The search for the bone of Luz of Jewish mythology ("the only one which withstands dissolution after death, out of which the body will be developed at the resurrection")[15] came to occupy him almost to the exclusion of other interests. "The form of the bone is really similar to that of an almond," he explains in a note to "Death's Jest Book."[16] Beddoes had meanwhile formed a close relationship with a young Russian Jewish student named Bernhard Reich, with whom he lived for a year, and whom some have tentatively identified as the "loved, long-lost boy."[17] Beddoes's note continues: "Mr. Reich to whom I am obliged for the above intends to publish shortly an academical disquisition on the subject, which, enriched as it will be, with many very ingenious suppositions and curious discussions on the philosophy and language of the Jews and other orientals, will form a very acceptable Essay towards the history of the remarkable doctrine [of the] resurrection, and many other points of Judaical physiology & [religion]."[18]

Unfortunately, there exists no trace of the disquisition and no further trace of Reich himself after the year he spent with Beddoes, so it is impossible to know the precise nature of their relationship or its effect on Beddoes's thought.

Beddoes's later years, though poorly documented, seem to have become increasingly turbulent. Several times disciplined for drunken and disorderly behavior, he also became active in radical German politics of the 1830s, and was perhaps the only foreigner to be admitted to the Germania Burschenschaft, a radical student organization. A pleasant stay of seven years in Zurich, during which he produced and starred in an acclaimed performance of both parts of Shakespeare's *Henry IV,* ended with his expulsion on political grounds. During his last years, his companion was a young baker, who subsequently became an actor of note, named Konrad Degen, described as "a nice-looking young man, nineteen years of age, dressed in a blue blouse, and of a natural dignity of manner."[19] In June 1848, Beddoes left Degen in Frankfurt and returned a last time to Switzerland, where he put up at the Cigogne Hotel in Basel; the next morning, he cut open an artery in his leg with a razor. Eventually gangrene set in; the leg was amputated below his knee. Finally on January 26, 1849, he succeeded in taking his life with poison, having written the same day to his executor, Revell Phillips: "I am food for *what I am good for—* worms," adding, "I ought to have been among other things a good poet; Life was too great a bore on one peg & that a bad one."[20]

In 1850, "Death's Jest Book" was finally published, thanks to the efforts of the faithful Kelsall, who subsequently bequeathed his box of Beddoes's manuscripts to Browning. The latter had declared himself an enthusiastic fan: "The power of the man is immense and irresistible," he wrote Kelsall.[21] Browning had intended to edit a critical edition of Beddoes's poetry, but for various reasons—including, apparently, his belated discovery of Beddoes's suicide—never got around to doing so. Instead, he entrusted the task to Edmund Gosse, who published a two-volume collection of Beddoes's poetry in 1890. Meanwhile, the box of manuscripts devolved to Browning's son and eventually disappeared. Fortunately, careful copies of most of them had been made by another admirer, but an authoritative edition of Beddoes would have to wait until 1935. The 1890 edition seems to have attracted little notice, since Lytton Strachey could ask in 1907 in "The Last Elizabethan," the first important piece of criticism of Beddoes: "How many among Apollo's pew-renters, one wonders, have ever read Beddoes, or, indeed, have ever heard of him?" And he points to a curious paradox:

If the neglect suffered by Beddoes's poetry may be accounted for in more ways than one, it is not so easy to understand why more curiosity has never been aroused by the circumstances of his life. For one reader who cares to concern himself with the intrinsic merit of a piece of writing there are a thousand who are ready to explore with eager sympathy the history of the writer; and all that we know both of the life and character of Beddoes possesses those very qualities of peculiarity, mystery and adventure, which are so dear to the hearts of subscribers to circulating libraries.[22]

And it is true that Beddoes's deliciously cautionary life has
scarcely done the trick for him even now. After Donner's
definitive biography and *Collected Works* of the mid-1930s,
little critical heed has been taken of Beddoes. Apparently he
wasn't mad enough or pathetic enough to have inspired the
outpouring of critical concern accorded Clare in the 1960s
and down to the present. There have been exceptions:
Harold Bloom's pages on Beddoes in *The Visionary Com-
pany;* Northrop Frye's in *A Study of English Romanticism;*
and a somewhat more extensive discussion in Eleanor
Wilner's 1975 book, *Gathering the Winds.* Recently—and
most usefully—there has been James R. Thompson's mono-
graph in the Twayne series. But the poetry is again largely
inaccessible. A slim selection published by Carcanet in the
1970s was supplanted by a more substantial one in 1999,
but Donner's complete edition and a smaller one he pub-
lished in 1950 are all but unfindable in rare book shops (the
complete was reprinted in an edition for libraries by AMS in
1978). Under the circumstances, it is still difficult for readers
of poetry to know whether or not the case presents a signifi-
cant "adjunct to the muses' diadem."

In my opinion it does. My first acquaintance with Beddoes
happened shortly after my undergraduate days when I found
a copy of Gosse's 1890 collection. My admiration originally
was for "Dream-Pedlary" and a few other short, beautifully
chiseled lyrics. The minuscule type in this edition drove me
away from the dramas, which looked hopelessly unkempt
anyhow. Not until the relatively commodious pages of Don-
ner's Muses' Library edition could I begin to come to terms

with them, and that not immediately. For as a reader soon discovers, the gold in Beddoes is inextricably entangled in the ore of the plays. It is not just that he is a "poet of fragments"; it is that the fragments don't separate easily from the matrix, and when they do, something is found wanting: they need their rough natural setting to register fully, even as it partially obscures them. There is no way, really, except to sign for the whole bill of goods and hope that prospecting will turn out to be worth the trouble. After which we may well come to agree with Gosse's estimate in his 1890 preface: "At the feast of the muses he appears bearing little except one small savory dish, some cold preparation, we may say, of olives and anchovies, the strangeness of which has to make up for its lack of importance. Not every palate enjoys this *hors d'oeuvre,* and when that is the case, Beddoes retires; he has nothing else to give. He appeals to a few literary epicures, who, however, would deplore the absence of this oddly flavored dish as much as that of any more important *pièce de résistance.*"[23]

I'd like to return to John Clare for a minute, because I could start to characterize Beddoes by first pointing to a kind of poetry absolutely unlike his. There is a short poem of Clare's which exemplifies what it is in him that I find endlessly fascinating. It's called "Mouse's Nest."

> I found a ball of grass among the hay
> And proged it as I passed and went away
> And when I looked I fancied somthing stirred
> And turned agen and hoped to catch the bird
> When out an old mouse bolted in the wheat

With all her young ones hanging at her teats
She looked so odd and so grotesque to me
I ran and wondered what the thing could be
And pushed the knapweed bunches where I stood
When the mouse hurried from the crawling brood
The young ones squeaked and when I went away
She found her nest again among the hay
The water oer the pebbles scarce could run
And broad old cesspools glittered in the sun.[24]

Here is Clare on his rounds again, telling us what he has just seen but neglecting to mention why he thinks it ought to interest us or even him. Though he has been likened to Burns, there is no suggestion implicit or otherwise that the sight of this "wee, sleekit, cowrin', tim'rous beastie" has stirred Clare to reflections on his own unsatisfactory condition or that of mankind in general; there is not even a sign that Clare's mouse is cowrin' and tim'rous. Clare just happened by; before he recognized the creature as a mouse, he thought she looked odd and grotesque. Subsequently he saw no occasion to revise his estimate and even less to humanize or allegorize her. Instead, after noting that she found her nest again, his attention turns, as the poem is signing off, to the undistinguished landscape. The water is having difficulty making its way over the pebbles. It must be a dry summer. The only hint of grandeur in the closure is the appearance of the cesspools—broad, old, glittering, they have their dignity under the sun, even though most travelers would hurriedly pass them by with pinched noses. And the poem is done. Clare was here—he saw what there was to see and noted it down, then went about his business of idle observation, ready to collect further swatches of nature as casually as one might pick a wildflower, press it between the pages of a book, and forget it.

Here is Beddoes reporting on what he saw, presumably on an outing:

> Hard by the lilied Nile I saw
> A duskish river-dragon stretched along,
> The brown habergeon of his limbs enamelled
> With sanguine almandines and rainy pearl:
> And on his back there lay a young one sleeping;
> No bigger than a mouse; with eyes like beads,
> And a small fragment of its speckled egg
> Remaining on its harmless, pulpy snout;
> A thing to laugh at, as it gaped to catch
> The baulking merry flies. In the iron jaws
> Of the great devil-beast, like a pale soul
> Fluttering in rocky hell, lightsomely flew
> A snowy trochilus, with roseate beak
> Tearing the hairy leeches from his throat.[25]

Even making allowances for the exotic locale, this passage is fairly typical of Beddoes's customary way of depicting nature. Though he, like Clare, was fond of going on walking trips in the country, there is never a hint that what he saw there was of any use or interest to him. Nature is exclusively literary for Beddoes. The omnipresent flowers in his poems, especially roses, sick ones if possible, are there to remind us of the nearness of death, of its consequences which will leave us "turning to daisies gently in the grave."[26] The smells of nature—Clare's cesspools, for instance—are here attar of roses and the stench of rotting flesh. The imagery is precious, enamelled; the message is either horrific or unconvincingly transcendental. I find both kinds of poetry necessary; my own has swung—on its own, I might add—always between the poles of Clare's lumpy poetry of mud and muck and Beddoes's perfumed and poisonous artifice, like the poisoned bouquet that Lenora, in "The Bride's Tragedy," gives her daughter's murderer. "Here are all colours / That bloomed the fairest in her heavenly face," she says, offering the bouquet, and after it has been accepted remembers to add that she "steeped the plants in a magician's potion, / More deadly than the scum of Pluto's pool . . . / One drop of it, poured in a city conduit, / Would ravage wider than a year of plague."[27] Nature exists to remind us of our mortality; the more poisonous the flowers, the better, and though Beddoes excels at portraying instantaneous Shelleyan (Shelley was his favorite modern poet) landscapes, fixed as though in a flash of lightning, their loveliness is neither comforting nor even neutral, but an invitation to death.

"The Bride's Tragedy" is the first and shapeliest of Beddoes's dramas, as well as his first significant piece of writing, and his farewell to conventional playwriting, though even here, "conventional" is a relative term. It was well received and seemed to announce a successful career for the eighteen-year-old author. One critic wrote: "The management of the plot is very inartificial and unskillful, as might be expected from so young a writer, and the dialogue . . . is nearly all entirely inappropriate . . . but regarded as poetry alone, it is

. . . of a degree of originality and beauty which even these most poetical days rarely present."[28] The central episode in the complicated plot is the murder of young Floribel by her hitherto seemingly doting fiancé, Hesperus. His motive is threefold: he must save his father from prison by marrying another woman; he is jealous of an innocent kiss Floribel bestowed on a pageboy; and he is subject to periodic fits of madness. But this abundance of motives in fact leaves Hesperus motiveless; the suspicion remains that he might easily have found another, harmless way out of his difficulties, that he kills merely because he is a character in a Beddoes play. The final scene of the play out-hecatombs *Hamlet;* most of the principal characters are either dead or wandering off in search of death. Floribel's mother, as noted, appears at the end with her poisoned bouquet just before Hesperus is to be executed. Her motive is to save her daughter's lover from the indignity of a public execution, a thoughtful gesture as unreal as Hesperus' motivation for the murder. Finally, it seems as though no one has any motives, that the protagonists behave arbitrarily according to how Beddoes pulls the strings. Their characters are hardly limned at all; they all speak Beddoes's sequined poetry; even unnamed characters have memorable speeches cut from the same length of goods. A character named Hubert is introduced mainly so that he can discover Floribel's grave and comment on the weather, which is always going from bad to worse. The result is less a play than a series of monologues which rarely mesh; as will be the case with Beddoes's subsequent dramatic efforts, there is no central norm of sanity to give relief to the characters' villainous insanity, no vortex at the center of the swirling maelstrom of poetry. Yet the end result is somehow theatrically effective, even though Beddoes has ignored most rules of the theater. This was to be the method of his stagecraft as it would culminate in "Death's Jest Book."

"Torrismond" is the next substantial dramatic fragment. The plot deals with a father's mistaken repudiation of his son, Torrismond, with the expected earth-shattering results. At the end of the act, Torrismond is racing toward death as Hesperus did, and determined to travel there first-class: "We'll drive in a chariot to our graves, / Wheel'd with big thunder, o'er the heads of men."[29] The three acts of "The Second Brother" deal with a conflict between two brothers, Orazio and Marcello. Returning after years of wandering to his native Ferrara, Marcello is mistaken for a beggar and is rudely snubbed by the handsome, hedonistic Orazio. Beddoes's characters frequently use far lesser pretexts as grounds for murder, and Marcello promptly turns into a vengeful fiend from hell, seizing the dukedom from his sibling and casting him into a dungeon; the fragment closes with what appear to be plans for further refinements of Marcello's scheme for cosmic revenge.

All of these splintered works are rehearsals for "Death's Jest Book," the astounding bottomless pit which absorbed all of Beddoes's creative energies during the more than two decades till his death. For a detailed summary of the plot, interested parties are referred to the lucid account of it in James R. Thompson's monograph. As he says, the play is dramatic, "but dramatic in the sense that [it] becomes a great stage on which Beddoes can act out, explore, and assess all his feelings and ideas, a place where he can test approaches to life through role playing, a means of articulating his troubled vision."[30] Another critic observes that the characters have "the essential unity of dream characters" who meet "in the dreamer" and are merely "emanations of the central idea."[31] In such a situation, a summary of the action provides us with a view of the multiple self-generated projections of the characters colliding with each other; the end product is chaos with a point. For that very reason, it seems important to trace the convolutions of the plot.

Roughly, the play deals with a series of betrayals and counter-betrayals among three sets of brothers: Melveric, Duke of Münsterberg, and his blood-brother Wolfram; Wolfram and his genetic brother Isbrand, the chief villain in a cast so crowded with them that it is difficult to know whom to sympathize with least; and Melveric's two sons, Athulf and Adalmar. Other characters are a "zany," Homunculus Mandrake, who is called on occasionally for comic relief; Ziba, a sinister Egyptian slave; Siegfried, Isbrand's confidant; and two more or less interchangeable heroines, Sibylla and Amala, who, like all of Beddoes's female characters, are passive and exhausted, eager for the death which will arrive all too soon. The action begins in Ancona, where Wolfram is about to set off on a mission to Africa to rescue the Duke from infidel captors, despite the fact that, as Wolfram's brother Isbrand reminds him, Melveric had murdered their father and usurped the ducal throne. Once arrived in Africa, Wolfram no sooner rescues the Duke than the latter murders him, jealous of the attachment between Wolfram and Sibylla, whom Melveric had rescued from captivity and in whom he seems to lose interest once he has dispatched

Wolfram: this is one of several instances in the play where someone murders the person who has just saved his life, and but one of many instances of unexpected and unnatural reactions, which by the end of the play have accumulated to a point where it is no longer possible to discern motives, plausible or otherwise. Isbrand, left in Ancona to meditate revenge on the Duke for murdering his father, muses: "Cheer up. Art thou alone? Why so should be / Creators and destroyers."[32] With the return of the Duke, disguised as a pilgrim, Isbrand, disguised as a court fool, now has an additional motive, as though any were needed, to seek revenge: the Duke's murder of Wolfram. But as readers of Marston and Webster, two of Beddoes's favorite dramatists, will know, mere murder in such a setting is an insufficient revenge. Through a series of complicated maneuvers, Isbrand eventually succeeds in having the Duke bring back to earth the shade of murdered Wolfram instead of the dead wife he had hoped to resurrect. Henceforth, Wolfram's ghost plays an active role, and though fairly benevolent for a ghost, at the end he summons the Duke to follow him living into the underworld: for once the Duke obeys docilely. Meanwhile, Athulf, in love with Amala, who is betrothed to Adalmar but secretly loves Athulf, has taken poison. Adalmar attempts to help him and discovers that the poison is a harmless drug, whereupon Athulf stabs his brother for his pains. Sibylla has promised to die so as to join Wolfram among the shades, and does so; Isbrand, having overthrown the government and made himself ruler, is stabbed by a minor character; and Athulf, having barely escaped a self-inflicted death by poison, stabs himself at the sight of Adalmar's funeral procession.

Another reason the chaotic plot matters is the magnificent language the characters use to cloak or explicate their more or less incomprehensible actions. Somewhere, somehow, Beddoes as in all his work is trying to make a point about death, but he never succeeds in doing so. Is death to be desired because it brings peace? Apparently not, judging from the swarms of demons and devils awaiting the miscreants. Yet despite his apparent belief in these, he remains an atheist: God is seldom mentioned, and the possibility of a Christian afterlife not at all. The most fortunate alternative will be turning to daisies gently in the grave. But since this will happen anyway, what's all the fuss about? In truth there is no rhyme or reason to Beddoes's death-haunted universe; one can end up feeling that he just likes talking about death, that the sound of the word is comforting, and that further comfort is beside the point. Thompson makes a game attempt to unravel Beddoes's philosophy, but is it worth it? Strachey says that Beddoes belongs to "the class of writers of which, in English literature, Spenser, Keats and Milton are the dominant figures—the writers who are merely great because of their art. Sir James Stephen was only telling the truth when he remarked that Milton might have put all that he had to say in *Paradise Lost* into a prose pamphlet of two or three pages. But who cares about what Milton had to say? It is his way of saying it that matters; it is his expression."[33]

Granted that "it is in [Beddoes's] expression that his greatness lies," as Strachey argues. It is still difficult to fathom the nature of that expression, isolate the components of its peculiar enchantment; to know what to do with his brilliant fragments, embedded as they so often are in the magma of an

impossible dramatic structure. Take for instance this frag-
ment relating to Ziba, not the character in "Death's Jest
Book," but another of the same name in the group of frag-
ments from an earlier play, "Love's Arrow Poisoned."
"Ziba / Was born in an old ruined century / Three or four
doors above the one we live in."[34] An observation like this
brings one up short, and therefore is hardly suited to an
ongoing dramatic flow. "Hey, wait a minute," one wants to
ask, "what exactly is this old ruined century that's a mere
three or four doors above ours? How did it get there? How
did we get here? And what kind of person is this Ziba?"
Somehow he seems menacing, even though he has done
nothing worse, as far as we know, than being born three or
four doors from us. Even the name—a female-sounding one,
yet belonging to a male slave—seems to contain a drop of
that essence of evil, heightened by its isolation in a single line
atop the other two lines of the fragment. And what of that
other molten line from the same group of fragments: "Like
the red outline of beginning Adam"? Or still another: "These
are as many / As bird-roads in the air"? Or this: "The swan-
winged horses of the skies / With summer's music in their
manes"?[35] Each of these is a potential show-stopper and
implies the question "Where do we go from here?" Why not
just stay here, trying to plumb the seemingly bottomless
meaning of these fragments that are scarcely even chips?

If Beddoes's plays were to be staged, they would require a
specially trained audience, no doubt, since the practical
questions they pose are "though puzzling . . . yet not beyond
all conjecture."[36] Strachey points out that "it is precisely
upon the stage that such faults of construction as those

which disfigure Beddoes' tragedies matter least. An audience, whose attention is held and delighted by a succession of striking incidents clothed in splendid speech, neither cares nor knows whether the effect of the whole, as a whole, is worthy of the separate parts."[37] Just as this unprepared public might be the ideal one for Beddoes's plays, so twentieth-century readers are prepared in advance to deal with the poetry: fragments shored against our ruin. Eliot's and subsequent fragmentations in poetry have shown us how to deal with fragments: by leaving them as they are, at most intuiting a meaning from their proximity to each other, but in general leaving it at that. The poetry is complete as it stands, and to wish a further completeness for it would be to destroy its tough but fragile essence.

I feel I should not close without giving one of Beddoes's poems in full, one of that handful which are not fragments but unflawed crystals, and the obvious choice is "Dream-Pedlary"; even though it is Beddoes's most famous poem, many do not know it. George Saintsbury thought that it "should be universally known," adding, "what words can possibly do justice to its movement and music?"[38] Donner, who spent seven pages analyzing its metrical complications, which are legion despite its deceptive simplicity, said that "all the elements of poetry were here forged together and remain inseparable: meaning, words and metre, all the constituents of poetry, are united into one whole which is the poem itself."[39] As for me, I've contemplated it for many years without feeling that I've plumbed its formal intricacies or its ambivalent message, yet both, as I said, appear at first glance to be crystal-clear.

"Dream-Pedlary"

1

If there were dreams to sell,
  What would you buy?
Some cost a passing bell;
  Some a light sigh,
That shakes from Life's fresh crown
Only a rose-leaf down.
If there were dreams to sell,
Merry and sad to tell,
And the crier rung the bell,
  What would you buy?

2

A cottage lone and still,
  With bowers nigh,
Shadowy, my woes to still,
  Until I die.
Such pearl from Life's fresh crown
Fain would I shake me down.
Were dreams to have at will,
This would best heal my ill,
  This would I buy.

3

But there were dreams to sell,
  Ill didst thou buy;
Life is a dream, they tell,
  Waking, to die.
Dreaming a dream to prize,

Is wishing ghosts to rise;
    And, if I had the spell
    To call the buried, well,
       Which one would I?

    4

If there are ghosts to raise,
    What shall I call,
Out of hell's murky haze,
    Heaven's blue hall?
Raise my loved longlost boy
To lead me to his joy.
    There are no ghosts to raise;
    Out of death lead no ways;
      Vain is the call.

    5

Know'st thou not ghosts to sue?
    No love thou hast.
Else lie, as I will do,
    And breathe thy last.
So out of Life's fresh crown
Fall like a rose-leaf down.
    Thus are the ghosts to woo;
    Thus are all dreams made true;
      Ever to last![40]

III

The Bachelor Machines of Raymond Roussel

In 1951, my friend Kenneth Koch returned from a year's Fulbright scholarship in Paris with a number of odd-looking French books in his luggage. By far the oddest-looking of these was a book-length poem entitled *Nouvelles Impressions d'Afrique* by a writer I'd never heard of, Raymond Roussel. The binding had a nineteenth-century look, and indeed the publisher, Lemerre, included a list on the back cover of volumes by once-illustrious nineteenth-century French poets like Leconte de Lisle, François Coppée, and José-María de Hérédia. Inside, the text was interrupted every few pages by an illustration in a fluent but utterly conventional style that reminded me of illustrations in a French conversation book I'd had in school. But if the style was conventional, the subjects were strange: a snowman in a solitary landscape; a shutter banging in the wind; a blindfolded military officer about to face the firing squad; a woman peering through the slits of a Venetian blind; a prosperous-looking elderly gent seated at a desk, holding a revolver to his temple. What kind of narrative poem could possibly link together this group of totally unrelated images?

But it was the text itself that looked oddest of all. The poem was divided into four sections or cantos, each of which bore the title of a monument or curiosity presumably to be found in Africa. The first was "Damietta: The House Where Saint Louis Was Kept Prisoner." The poem was in seemingly regular alexandrines, but constantly interrupted by parentheses, which were in turn interrupted by double, triple, quadruple, and even quintuple parentheses. In fact, each canto consisted of a single fairly short sentence expanded to epic length by the accordion-like system of parentheses. There were footnotes as well, also in rhyming alexandrines and with their own sets of parentheses. Decidedly curious. At the time, I believe I made a mental note to someday learn enough French to be able to read the poem, if only to find out what it could possibly be about.

This wasn't to happen for a number of years. In 1958, after two years in France as a Fulbright scholar and another year in New York taking graduate courses in French at New York University, I decided to go back to France and try to collect material for a dissertation on Roussel. In part, this was a pretext to extract money from my parents so that I could go on living in Paris, which had agreed with me. But I did do some research on Roussel, even after abandoning the project of a dissertation.

At the time, Roussel was an all-but-forgotten figure, despite the fact that he had been championed by the Surrealists, cited by Marcel Duchamp as the determining influence on his later art and on his still-later vocation of chess, and played an as yet unrecognized role in the formulation of the then-fashionable *nouveau roman,* whose chief practitioners,

Alain Robbe-Grillet and Michel Butor, were aware of Roussel's work and had published little-noticed essays on it.[1] For once, being an American in Paris was actually an advantage. For though I earned a brief notoriety as *"ce fou d'Américain qui s'intéresse à Raymond Roussel,"* I was successful in approaching Roussel's nephew, the Duc d'Elchingen, who had always considered his uncle the skeleton in the family closet and systematically refused any contact with French writers who sought to interview him on that subject. During our first meeting, he asked me if I thought Roussel's work might have the same success in America as Françoise Sagan's. My reply of "why not?" was enough to grant me access to whatever materials the Duc possessed—not much, as it turned out, beyond snapshots in family albums. Papers were rare, and no doubt the Duc, whose uncle was, among other things, a homosexual drug addict who had squandered an immense family fortune partly by sparing no expense in publishing his works and producing his incomprehensible plays, had not been much moved to preserve what there was.[2]

There were other cold trails to follow. By chance, I traced Roussel's official mistress to a nursing home in Brussels, thanks to a man at her previous address who happened to remember where she had gone. Through chance acquaintances, I met maternal relatives of Roussel whose existence I hadn't known of; through the art critic Max Kozloff, I met the hitherto untraceable widow of Pierre Frondaie, who had adapted one of Roussel's novels for the stage: Kozloff just happened to be renting an apartment in her suburban home. A friend found a copy of the auction catalogue of Roussel's mother's important art collection at a Paris flea market. The

Surrealist painter Jacques Hérold, I discovered, owned a galley proof that turned out to be the missing introductory chapter of an unfinished novel by Roussel that had been published posthumously. The chapter was at that time the first unpublished work of his ever to surface.

By the early sixties, the trails were starting to heat up. In 1963, Michel Foucault published his first book, a critical study of Roussel called *Death and the Labyrinth*.[3] Shortly thereafter, the magazine *Bizarre* devoted an entire issue to Roussel, to which I contributed an essay on Roussel's plays.[4] The publisher Jean-Jacques Pauvert acquired the rights to Roussel's works and began reissuing them; meanwhile, the firm of Gallimard, unaware of this, brought out Roussel's long out-of-print novel *Locus Solus* and was forced by Pauvert to withdraw it. I published the first American study of Roussel in *Art News Annual* in 1961,[5] which was included shortly thereafter in an Italian collection of essays on him; in England, the novelist Rayner Heppenstall published a book-length study of Roussel and, in collaboration with his daughter, a translation of *Impressions d'Afrique*.[6] Meanwhile, Roussel's nephew the Duc was giving interviews to anyone who cared to listen, and in 1972 a biography by François Caradec appeared, incorporating all the meager knowledge of Roussel's life known at the time.[7] The Roussel industry was under way.

Today, Roussel's work, mass-marketed in pocket editions, has become fodder for critics everywhere—it seems to have been written in order to be deconstructed—and it is also discussed on television and in glossy magazines. Conferences on his work are held regularly in Nice, a city that plays an important role in his early work, and during at least one of these, the participants were served one of Roussel's favorite dishes, chocolate soup, made from a recipe recently divulged by his former chef. It is possible that if he were alive he might feel he had finally achieved the fame for which he always felt himself destined, though the reasons for it might surprise him. Much of it, in fact, stems from the vast corpus of anecdotes, real and apocryphal, surrounding his life, which he tried to keep as secret as possible.

Another reason for the work's latter-day critical success is the ease with which it can, as the French say, be served with every kind of sauce. From Jean Cocteau to Foucault and beyond, critics who discuss Roussel tend almost unconsciously to write about themselves. What can Roussel do for me, how will he affect me, is the unspoken premise of much of it. Cocteau's appreciation of Roussel in *Opium* is valuable, especially since they were fellow pensioners at the same detoxification clinic in St. Cloud, but his confession that "in 1918 I rejected Roussel as likely to place me under a spell from which I could see no escape. Since then I have constructed defenses. I can look at him from the outside"[8] sets the tone for much of what was to follow.

There is no doubt that Roussel left a good deal of work for the critic willing to take it on, and there are now many of these. For instance, a recent study by Philippe G. Kerbellec is devoted entirely to unraveling the puns that were an integral part of Roussel's "method" of writing, and of which he gave a few examples in his posthumous text *Comment j'ai écrit certains de mes livres (How I Wrote Certain of My Books)*.[9]

No one denies that Roussel's work is brimming with secrets; what is less certain is whether the secrets have any importance. In other words, is there some hidden, alchemical key for decoding the work, as André Breton and others have thought, or is the hidden meaning merely the answer to a childish riddle or puzzle, no more nor less meaningful than the context in which it is buried? These questions are unlikely to be resolved. Meanwhile, to make them the focus of a critical inquiry into Roussel's work is to risk diluting the very glamour that brings readers to that work in the first place. Caradec says, "We must read the work first and foremost for what it is, a marvelous game that enchants us."[10]

In order to look at the work, we must start by examining the life, not least because in this case the life is to a large extent the work: first because of the overriding importance of his work for Roussel himself—it seems to have crowded all but the most superficial personal relationships out of his life; second because of the paucity of biographical materials. Caradec's 1972 biography is in fact largely a collection of Roussel's postcard greetings, thank-you notes, and dedications he signed in his books, interspersed with excerpts from reviews of his plays and the rare reviews his books received during his lifetime. (A vastly augmented revised version, taking account of the recent discoveries of Roussel material, was published in 1997.) To an unusual degree, the man has melted into the silhouette of the author.

Roussel was born in Paris on January 20, 1877, to affluent parents: his father, Eugène, was a stockbroker; his mother, Marguerite, was the daughter of a wealthy Paris business-

man. They lived at 25 Boulevard Malesherbes, near the
Madeleine Church, and were thus neighbors of the family of
Marcel Proust, who lived at number 9. We know that Rous-
sel and Proust knew each other, since later in life Roussel
used a somewhat patronizing compliment from Proust in the
publicity brochures that accompanied his books; and there
are a few references to the Roussel family in Proust's letters.
(Roussel is a not uncommon name in France, hence they may
refer to another family; but one that definitely pertains to
Raymond's is an allusion to his sister as "la petite Roussel"
in a letter telling of her engagement to the Prince de la
Moskowa.) The Roussels also knew the painter Madeleine
Lemaire, the principal model for Proust's Mme. Verdurin,
who painted a portrait of Raymond as a child. Later in life,
Roussel became acquainted with Robert de Montesquiou,
Proust's Baron de Charlus, who wrote one of the first sub-
stantial critical essays on Roussel's work. Resemblances be-
tween the character and writing of Proust and Roussel have
often been noted, and from certain aspects Roussel looks like
a ghostly reflection of Proust; Roger Vitrac, for instance,
called him "the Proust of dreams."[11] Yet in spite of these tan-
talizing tangents, we know very little of Roussel's life in
Parisian high society, if indeed there was any.

In the 1880s, the Roussels moved from the Boulevard
Malesherbes to a splendid mansion just off the Champs-
Elysées; they also spent time at a villa in the Bois de Boulogne
at Neuilly and later summered in another villa overlooking
the Atlantic at Biarritz. Raymond was allowed to leave the
lycée to study piano at the Paris Conservatory, where his

performances of difficult works such as Liszt's études, Chopin's scherzos, and Balakirev's *Islamey* were praised by his professors and eventually won him a first honorable mention at the annual *concours*. When he was sixteen he composed songs, but gave these up for poetry a year later because he found that "the words came easier than the music."[12]

In *Comment j'ai écrit certains de mes livres*, Roussel tells us: "I would like to mention here a curious crisis I experienced at the age of nineteen, when I was writing *La Doublure* [his first substantial work, a novel in verse]. For several months I experienced a sensation of universal glory of an extraordinary intensity."[13] The crisis is described by the psychologist Pierre Janet, who treated Roussel, in his book *De l'Angoisse à l'Extase (From Anguish to Ecstasy)*: he quotes him as saying, "Something in particular makes you feel that you are creating a masterpiece, that you are a prodigy: there are child prodigies who reveal themselves at the age of eight; I was one who revealed himself at nineteen. I was the equal of Dante and Shakespeare; I felt what the aged Victor Hugo felt at seventy, what Napoleon felt in 1811, what Tannhäuser dreamed at the Venusberg: I felt glory." He goes on: "What I was writing radiated beams of light; I shut the curtains because I was afraid the slightest chink would let the beams from my pen escape outside. If I had left papers lying around, it would have produced rays of light that would have reached as far as China, and the bewildered crowd would have stormed the house . . . I lived more at that moment than in all the rest of my existence." Janet adds, "He would have given his whole life in order to find a moment of equal happiness."[14]

When *La Doublure* was published to no acclaim the fol-
lowing year, in 1899, and Roussel discovered that the sun
and moon were still in place, that the planets hadn't strayed
from their orbits and that daily life in Paris went on as
before, he sank into a profound state of depression that was
accompanied by a rash that covered most of his body; it was
apparently at that point that his parents sought the advice of
Pierre Janet. Although *La Doublure* was far from a master-
piece and Roussel's most important work lay in the future, it
was as if the game had ended there; any praise or blame his
future work might occasion would be beside the point.

One of the curious things about Roussel's work is how
little the early, middle, and late works resemble each other.
La Doublure and the book which followed it, *La Vue,* are
long poems in which rhymed descriptions of mundane
objects dominate almost to the exclusion of everything else.
These are the works which influenced the *nouveau roman,*
for example Alain Robbe-Grillet's *Le Voyeur* and *La Jalousie*
with their tedious descriptions of a Venetian blind or a
packet of Gauloises floating in the water. Roussel's next two
books are ostensibly novels, in prose this time. Here again
description is paramount, though it is description not of the
mundane but of fantastic scenes, inventions, curious works
of art: this is the work that affected Duchamp and later the
Surrealists. Although stage works were drawn from these
two novels, Roussel's theater proper consists of two plays
written in the 1920s: *L'Étoile au Front* and *La Poussière de
Soleils.* Both of these are merely collections of anecdotes that
the characters recount to each other; in the first, they are
engendered by the various items in a collection of curios; in

the second, by clues in a treasure hunt which lead to the discovery of a will. Just as the novels end up as novels in spite of everything (Cocteau said, "Ultimately, *Impressions of Africa* leaves an impression of Africa"),[15] the plays are dramatic in a way of their own: Robert Desnos commented that "the characters are tragically reduced to chess pieces controlled by a passion: curiosity, vice, love."

Nouvelles Impressions d'Afrique (*New Impressions of Africa*, 1932), the epic poem with the strange illustrations and bristling parentheses, is in a category of its own. Although Roussel had always been fascinated by stories within stories, what the French call a novel with drawers, here the situation is reduced to many sentences interlocking within a single sentence. By flattening the thing out, so to speak, that is by unraveling the parenthetical thoughts and arranging them in proper sequence, it is possible to read the poem and make perfect sense of it. (Roussel had considered making the reader's task somewhat easier by having the book printed in inks of different colors, a project never realized perhaps because of the expense involved: by this time his fortune was seriously depleted.) It is the construction, not the content, of the poem that is mysterious, and content is definitively upstaged by construction.

Roussel's last book, *Comment j'ai écrit certains de mes livres,* appeared shortly after his death by suicide in a Palermo hotel room in 1933. It is a hodgepodge containing the essay "How I Wrote Certain of My Books"; hitherto uncollected juvenilia; an extract from Janet called "The Psychological Characteristics of Ecstasy," which discusses Roussel under the pseudonym Martial, the first name of the central character in *Locus Solus;* an article from a chess journal describing a move invented by Roussel; and the final, unfinished novel which appears under the heading "Documents to Serve as a Framework."

The last is an extraordinary work; again it is a novel with drawers, but since Roussel suppressed the introductory chapter (there is even a note at the beginning of the story requesting the printer to do so),[16] it would be impossible to guess how the tales are interconnected if the chapter hadn't survived providentially. As it is, we now know that the beginning describes a club in Havana whose thirty members were charged with the mission of coming up with examples of the superiority of Europe over America. Since Roussel had finished only six of these "documents" at the time of his death, he chose to publish them as a collection of unrelated tales. His maniacal concern for concision, for using the fewest possible words to say what he had to say, had always been a preoccupation. In the two plays, this is carried to such extremes that it was difficult for the actors to memorize their speeches and for the audience to follow them, while the "Documents" are so concentrated that their density is new even for Roussel: they are like heavy water.

Such is the rough outline of Roussel's literary career. Of his life not much remains to be said, since for him at least it had ended at the age of nineteen. Of course, he continued to do the things expected of his class and nationality: military service and later a job behind the lines during the World War; travel; winters at Nice and summers at Biarritz; evenings at the theater with his ostensible mistress, Mme. Dufrène. The major events were no doubt the four productions of his plays staged between 1911 and 1927; these were unfortunately catastrophes which caused Roussel great pain and his family extreme embarrassment. Most of his time seems to have been given over to writing. After the death of his mother in 1911, he inherited the house in Neuilly and lived there in almost total isolation. His habit was to write during the mornings and to consume a single meal comprising break-fast, lunch, and dinner from early to late afternoon; these solitary repasts often included twenty-seven courses. He was then free to spend the evening at the theater, where, with the long-suffering Mme. Dufrène, he often attended the same spectacle night after night, always sitting in the same seat if possible. His tastes ran toward the popular comedies, operettas, and melodramas of the day, and to children's plays, which he attended with Mme. Dufrène and a little girl of her acquaintance. He spent enormous sums on clothes, which he threw away after only a few wearings; his favorite sensation was to be entirely clad in new clothing, which he likened to "walking on eggs."[17] At the same time, he had a horror of doing something he had never done before, and repeated ritualistic acts of daily life as compulsively as the resuscitated corpses in *Locus Solus,* who, thanks to a chemi-cal called Resurrectine, survived to repeat the most impor-tant act of their lives *ad infinitum.*

His travels were similarly eccentric. There is a story that his mother, notorious for her own eccentricities, invited a group of guests on a tour to India aboard a private yacht which contained her coffin. When they were a few miles from the coast, she caught sight of land and ordered the cap-tain to turn around immediately and sail back to France.

Raymond traveled around the world in 1920–21, but apparently saw very little since he spent most of the time in hotel rooms writing, even in Peking. From Melbourne he wrote to Mme. Dufrène: "There are two beach resorts near here called Brighton and Menton. It's really worth while to come so far so as to be able to make an excursion from Brighton to Menton, which I did."[18] In New York, he was about to enjoy the luxury of a bath, when he noticed a brochure announcing that every room in the vast hotel was equipped with a bathroom. This threw him into a rage since he felt that luxuries should be enjoyed only by the few, otherwise they were meaningless—this despite his reputation for extreme generosity.

Thus, though his life bears superficial resemblances to those of other foppish, futile members of the privileged class of his day, there are differences which make it almost undecodable as normal human behavior. A similar disparity isolates his writing from the rest of literature; it's almost as though it had a different molecular structure.

Although *La Doublure* will disappoint those who have first read the later, fantastic works, it is an extraordinary performance, and one can almost understand the author's unnatural euphoria at the time of writing it. The title, as everywhere in Roussel, is a word with two meanings: *doublure* can mean either "lining" (of a garment) or "understudy." Only the latter meaning is brought into play in this story of Gaspard, a third-rate actor employed as an understudy in a costume drama in a Paris theater. But there is perhaps a connection with an early tale, "Chiquenaude," where the word *doublure* occurs in the first line and is given another meaning in the last, even though or perhaps because Roussel explicitly cautions us against making any rapprochement between the two works. At least one reader, the playwright Roger Vitrac, has done so, however, and has concluded that the punning first and last sentences show "how poetry destroys itself through the figure of the moths sewn in the flannel which destroyed the trousers supposed to be invulnerable."[19]

Be that as it may, the plot of this rhyming novel of almost two hundred pages can be easily summarized. Gaspard falls in love with a kept woman, Roberte; with her money, they leave together for Nice where they mingle in the carnival at Mardi Gras. At that point, there ensues an almost mathematically exact description of the floats and costumes of the carnival that takes up three-quarters of the book. The lovers drift apart; back in Paris, Gaspard has a new and inferior job working the annual carnival at Neuilly (not far from the Roussels' property). In the last line, with the carnival going on all around him, Gaspard, alone, gazes up at the stars.

It's a sad and sordid little story, one that might have escaped from the drawer of a naturalist writer such as Émile Zola, the Goncourt brothers, or Charles-Louis Philippe, the author of *Bubu of Montparnasse*. The interest is in the telling. The nineteen-year-old author has a prodigious gift for spinning fluid alexandrines that are nevertheless far from being poetry but are instead exquisitely ordered rhymed prose. Roussel's purpose is not to tell a story—there barely is one—but to describe objects and décors as minutely as possible, in a medium that is both seamless and pedestrian. The work is all of a piece (and one understands how this massive uniformity could have excited Roussel as he was writing), but the proportions are all wrong: we are constantly being forced to dwell on scenes of little interest while the psychological underpinnings of a love story are all but absent. During a lovemaking sequence in a chair, Roussel describes the veins in Roberte's breasts and her disordered dishabille, and ends with the line, "The back of the chair has cracked several times"[20]—these are radical shifts of focus which will recur later on in Surrealist prose like Louis Aragon's *Le Paysan de Paris* as well as in the *nouveau roman* and even in today's minimalist fiction, but which are startling to find in 1897 in a collection of popular authors of the day. One ends both by admiring the precision of Roussel's descriptions and agreeing with his biographer Caradec when he says, "Roussel seems to have been totally devoid of spontaneous imagination." One could say the same thing of a camera.

La Vue, Roussel's second book, published in 1903, continues in the descriptive vein of *La Doublure.* Again, the title may be a *jeu de mots: la vue* could mean "the view" and also "the faculty of sight." Each of the three long poems which compose it consists of a meticulous, even microscopic, description: not, this time, of actual scenes but of printed illustrations of them. The first and title poem describes a tiny reproduction of a beach scene (perhaps the beach at Biarritz, visible from the Roussels' summer home), set in the handle of a souvenir penholder and visible through a tiny peephole. The second, "Le Concert," describes in similar agonizing detail a scene of a band concert engraved on the letterhead of a sheet of hotel stationery. The third, "La Source," which can mean both "spa" and "source," describes a scene on the label of a bottle of mineral water, and takes the typical Rous-selian form of a vast digression or parenthesis. At the begin-ning, the narrator is seated at a restaurant table having lunch; the other patrons of the restaurant, including a young couple who are whispering and laughing together, are briefly evoked; the poet then launches into a fifty-page description of the spa pictured on the label, this time providing psycho-logical as well as physical descriptions of the figures who people the scene. Only at the end do we return to the restau-rant, where a note of loss creeps in: the couple are "still whis-pering things which can't be overheard." And at the end of the title poem the objective tone startlingly disappears as the narrator evokes "le souvenir vivace et latent d'un été / Déjà mort, déjà loin de moi, vite emporté" ("the latent, undying memory of a summer / Already dead, already far from me, borne swiftly away").[21] In the brief autobiographical note attached to *Comment j'ai écrit certains de mes livres,* Rous-sel tells us: "I have a delightful memory of my childhood. I can say that I experienced several years of perfect happiness then."[22] We know from other sources that he refused in later life to go near certain places of which he had particularly happy childhood memories, among them St. Moritz and Aix-les-Bains. Here, his intense descriptions of similar vaca-tion spots, first transformed into printed illustrations which could suffer no change or decay, amounts perhaps to his own *Recherche du temps perdu.* At any rate, this is as close to confession as Roussel will ever get.

At the end of a review of Roussel's play *L'Étoile au Front* in 1924, Paul Eluard wrote in the review *La Révolution Sur-réaliste:* "May Raymond Roussel continue to show us everything which has not been. We are a small group for whom that reality alone matters." In his next book, *Impressions d'Afrique,* published in 1910, Roussel abandons any pretense of realism to turn his attention definitively toward "everything which has not been." Once again, however, the novel is made up almost entirely of descriptions, held together by the barest suggestion of a plot. A group of Europeans, including a number of actors and circus artists en route to a tour in South America, are stranded in Africa when their ship, the Lynceus (the name of the Argonaut whose keen vision allowed him to see through walls and to observe events taking place in heaven and hell), is sunk off the African coast. They are captured and held for ransom by a local despot, the emperor Talou. To while away the time until their ransom arrives, they devise an elaborate entertainment or gala, utilizing the various special talents of each member of the troupe, to be held on the day of their liberation. The first half of the book is a description of the gala, interspersed with accounts of rather horrifying executions of various of Talou's subjects who have incurred his wrath. The second half is an explanation of the curious events we have just witnessed, an explanation which turns out to be more baffling than the events themselves. In order to make things a bit easier for his readers, Roussel inserted a printed slip at the beginning of the book, advising readers "not initiated to the art of Raymond Roussel" (one wonders who the initiates were) to begin the book at page 212, read to page 455, and then go back to read pages 1 to 211.

It has been suggested that the title *Impressions d'Afrique* may well be another of Roussel's puns. "Impressions" may refer to printed matter (as in first impression, second impression, etc.) and *d'Afrique* could be broken down into *de fric,* or "of moolah," which would constitute Roussel's ironic view of himself as a wealthy author forced to pay for his own publications. The title of his next novel, *Locus Solus* (1912), might mean "lonely place" or "the only place." After the failure of the play drawn from it, the title became notorious and the subject of countless puns, some fairly indecent, which Roussel seemed to appreciate since he lists them in his brief autobiographical sketch.

Here again, exposition is followed by explanation. A prominent scientist and inventor, Martial Canterel, who bears some resemblance to both Jules Verne and the astronomer Camille Flammarion, both of whom Roussel admired passionately, has invited a group of guests to inspect the marvels he has created in the gardens of his suburban villa, Locus Solus. His inventions, described with an even more minute precision than usual, become increasingly complex. After an airborne jackhammer which is busily constructing a mosaic of teeth wherein a German cavalryman figures, we pass on to a huge glass "diamond" in which float a nude dancing girl, a hairless cat, and the preserved head of Danton. More embalming occurs in the long central episode, where we witness eight strange *tableaux vivants* taking place in different compartments of an enormous glass cage. Only afterwards do we learn that the figures in the *tableaux* are corpses kept alive by injections of Canterel's patented Resurrectine, which allows them only enough animation to act out the most crucial event of their lives. For example, the frivolous young Englishwoman, Ethelfleda Exley, who had succumbed to the fashion for mirrored fingernails but who had a horror of blood and the color red, fainted at the sight, mirrored in the half-moon of one of her nails, of a lantern in which, for reasons too complicated to summarize here, a red map of Europe had been set. Shocked, she will continually repeat the words: "*Dans la lunule . . . l'Europe entière . . . rouge . . . toute entière . . .*" ("In the half-moon . . . the whole of Europe . . . red . . . entirely red . . .").[23] The scene has been carefully restaged by Canterel in a refrigerated glass case where stagehands in furs, rather like the supposedly invisible stagehands in a Noh performance, assure the smooth operation of the endlessly repeated scene.

The total lack of success of these books caused Roussel to believe he was pursuing the wrong medium. He decided that the theater might prove a better vehicle for the "message" that nobody seemed to understand. After *Locus Solus,* he adapted *Impressions d'Afrique* for the stage; the resulting failure and ridicule were predictable, but at least a number of literati learned of his work from attending the performance. Among them were Guillaume Apollinaire, whose *Mamelles de Tirésias* followed a few years later, and Marcel Duchamp, who has said that the play helped him to abandon the post-impressionist style he had been working in and proceed on to his celebrated *machines célibataires,* or "bachelor machines," such as "The Bride Stripped Bare by Her Bachelors, Even."[24] Similarly, Alberto Giacometti once told me that he had been inspired to produce such early surreal works as *The Palace at Four A.M.* by his reading of *Locus Solus.*

Despite this decisive influence on some of the great creative minds of the age, Roussel still remained unknown to the general public. Sadly, this was to change after the war with the scandal of his later theatrical flops. Imagining that the play *Impressions d'Afrique* had failed because he lacked knowledge of stagecraft, he commissioned Pierre Frondaie, a novelist known for his successful adaptations of popular novels for the stage, to turn *Locus Solus* into a play. The result far eclipsed the disaster of *Impressions d'Afrique*. Frondaie, who was paid a huge sum (as were all those involved in the production), seems deliberately to have turned the book to ridicule; at any rate, his dramatization is absurd and bears little relation to Roussel's novel. The fact that enormous sums went into the production—fashionable Caligari-esque sets by Emile Bertin, costumes by Paul Poiret, and a cast including some of the most illustrious names in the French theater of the time—helped to create a public outcry: the actors and theater directors were attacked for their venality (Frondaie had wisely remained anonymous), and Roussel was accused of depriving honest but poor playwrights of their livelihood.

There was a similar response by critics to the two plays that Roussel, finally convinced to tackle the theater on his own, produced during the 1920s: *L'Étoile au Front* (*The Star on the Forehead*) and *La Poussière de Soleils* (*The Dust of Suns*). The former, made up entirely of anecdotes broken up and distributed among the cast, caused the most uproar, though it is one of Roussel's loveliest and most accessible works. At times the texture suggests the orchestrations of Anton von Webern, where a single concise motif is passed around among a group of instruments.

JOUSSAC: And he fell again into a coma?

TREZEL: As completely as before, which gave rise to a terrible
moral crisis in his sister. She could no longer ignore the truth:
reduced to leaving his work of adoption unfinished, Gimon,
through his dictated will, wished to make his son the heir . . .

JOUSSAC: To her detriment . . .

CLAUDE: And to that of her daughter, which affected her much
more, since she remained above all a mother.[25]

In the end, the stories succeed in casting a strange light on the
characters who tell them, and an effect of drama, or at least
of theatricality, is obtained.

In 1915, Roussel had begun writing a long poem, he tells
us, which he interrupted to write the two plays. After finish-
ing them, he again took up this work, *Nouvelles Impressions
d'Afrique* (more paid publications?), which was to be his last
completed work and possibly his masterpiece. Perhaps the
interrupted composition had some influence on the form,
which consists merely of one interruption after another; per-
haps it was the ultimate crystallization of Roussel's digres-
sions, which, like Cubism, show us an object seen in its
totality through a prismatic grill of fractured planes.

The first canto, "Damiette," begins with the narrator's
astonishment on viewing the very house where Louis IX,
Saint Louis, was kept prisoner for three months at the time
of the Crusades. Yet the historic event seems close in time
when the narrator begins to think about the antiquity of the
"crumbling marvels" so common in Egypt. In their presence,
he says, everything else seems to date from yesterday, for
example the family name whose bearer is so proud that he

knows perfectly—and here begins the first digression—the way the occupant of a light-filled apartment on the top floor of a tall house, a photographer, knows . . . but he's a mediocre photographer, though clever at concealing crow's-feet and pimples . . . this thought in turn suggests a digression on the power of the retoucher, immediately interrupted by the thought of a vain person posing for his photograph and wondering whether, if he forgets to hold his breath, the image will be blurred. From this springs an immense list of things people tend to worry about: the infant growing cross-wise in the womb wonders whether, at birth, he will be his mother's assassin. The flower beneath a tree, urinated on by someone who has eaten asparagus, wonders if its perfume will come back; the wall, beaten by an overexcited shutter in the wind, wonders what crime of conscience it has committed; the tourist arriving in Nice for a winter vacation wonders, with one eye on the thermometer, whether he will dress in linen. This thought engenders a footnote: to offer an overcoat to a winter visitor at Nice is like: —and there follows a list of gifts that are certain to be refused: an emetic to a sinner who has just taken communion; an aphrodisiac to a hanged man; a narcotic to an eager listener at a lecture, and so on. Only after these parentheses and others like them have opened and closed are we allowed to finish the first interrupted sentence, which lists other old things that seem new in contrast to the antiquities of Egypt: unornamented cathedrals; the proud menhir; the cromlech; the dolmen, beneath which the ground is always dry. And what about Saint Louis and his house? They got disposed of in the few lines at the beginning of the canto: No doubt one is led to reflect, Roussel has told us, when one learns that Saint Louis spent three months as a prisoner behind that door. Period.

The other African "curiosities" are given the same treatment: scarcely are they mentioned when the narrator carries us off on a whirlwind tour of almost entirely irrelevant free-association. The nominal subjects of the poem are not subjects; they are scarcely even pretexts for the lists of banalities promptly interrupted by further lists, until the canto jerks finally to a close that could have been anywhere. *Nouvelles Impressions* is thus an anomaly: a narrative poem without a subject, or almost. The real subject is its form: the hiccupping parenthetical passages that continually frustrate and sidetrack the reader, until, ready to expire like an exhausted laboratory rat in a maze, he finds himself miraculously at the end of his wanderings, though scarcely the wiser for them. And yet the scenery along the way has made its point, amounting to something like daily life as it is actually lived: boring and at the same time exciting in its unavoidability. As Robbe-Grillet says of Roussel: "The clarity, the transparency, exclude the existence of other worlds behind things, and yet we discover that we can't get out of this world. Everything is at a standstill, everything is always happening all over again." He argues: "Here we have the perfect reversal of what people agree to call a good writer: Raymond Roussel has nothing to say, and he says it badly."[26] One could quarrel with this. If "nothing" means a labyrinth of brilliant stories told only for themselves, then perhaps Roussel has nothing to say. Does he say it badly? Well, he writes like a mathematician: his prose, in the words of Michel Leiris, "is French prose as one is taught to write it in the manuals of lycées."[27] In other words, it is a totally neutral medium for the "nothing" he is telling us. One can't help recalling John Cage's remark, "I have nothing to say / and I am saying it / and that is / poetry / as I need it."[28] Like Cage, Roussel is a poet who is about to be a poet: He is always bringing us face to face with the very latest moment in our thinking: the now where anything can and must happen, the *Locus Solus* where writing begins.

▲ "Why Must You Know?"

The Poetry of
John Wheelwright

Laura Riding once wrote me an angry letter in response to
a letter of mine offering to send her a publication of hers
of which she no longer had a copy and of which I had
heard she was in need. She replied that although she was
indeed sorely in need of the said publication, she could
not accept it from me. One reason seemed to be that I had
had the effrontery in an interview to state that I thought
her poetry had influenced mine, which she felt couldn't
possibly be the case. The chief one, however, was that I
had included her, along with John Wheelwright, the sub-
ject of this chapter, and David Schubert, who is to be the
subject of my last chapter, in a choice of what I felt were
important neglected twentieth-century poets for the mag-
azine *Poetry Pilot*. She accused me of "lumping me with a
group of poor creatures who, you say, have not received
their due."

Only recently did I discover that Wheelwright had writ-
ten a largely negative review of two of Riding's collections
of poetry, *A Joking Word* and *Laura and Francisca*, which
was published in *Poetry* (Chicago). Knowing Riding's
diligence in tracking down even the most ephemeral and
well-intentioned remarks on her work and taking their

authors to task in long letters to the editor, I felt that Wheelwright's article surely must have had some bearing on her assessment of him, more than forty years later, as a "poor creature." My reason for citing the review, however, is that Wheelwright's evaluation of Riding's poetry makes it sound strangely like his own, and therefore it seems a good place to begin a discussion of him. Poets, as has often been noted, in writing about other poets tend to write about themselves, even to the point of seeing as faults in others what they take to be virtues in themselves.

"Automatic writing," says Wheelwright (and here one should note that Riding's poetry in both intention and effect is about as far from automatic writing as one could get),

is a therapeutic exercise for writers and readers because it uncovers otherwise unrecoverable layers of the mind. But the ultimate esthetic value of such discoveries depends entirely on the intrinsic validity of the thought which is expressed. A great deal of thoughtful poetry is obscure. Any understanding of it is accompanied by the pleasant and flattering sensation of the intuitive unravelling of a puzzle. The result is always more enjoyable (or at least differently enjoyable) than work which addresses itself immediately to rational understanding. It is fun to recognize friends in masquerade. There is fun in masquerade itself, even though personages, when recognized, turn out to be enemies or bores, or to be scarcely persons at all.[1]

This is a most unfair characterization of Laura Riding by a poet as radically modernist as she. To many of Wheelwright's critics, however, it would have sounded like a fair assessment of him. From his very first appearance between book covers, in the 1923 anthology *Eight More Harvard Poets* (which gave rise to a parody anthology called *Eight Most Harvard Poets*), he was taxed, and rightly so, with obscurity. One early critic wrote of him: "He leaves the mind in a state bordering on collapse." (Wheelwright later used this quotation along with a sheaf of others, favorable and unfavorable, in a brochure he had printed to advertise his work.)[2] Yet almost all his poems carry an ideological freight which he sincerely meant to be understood: in the beginning the message was theological; toward the end, Marxist and revolutionary. Alan Wald, in his book *The Revolutionary Imagination*, says that "when Jack's political friends complained that his poems were incomprehensible, he conceded that they might be difficult but insisted they were not obscure. In a 1938 essay in *Partisan Review*, he pointed out that an authentic revolutionary poem might recognize 'mysteries and wrestle with them, which is a different matter from wilful mystification, although indistinguishable to persons who have stultified their interior resources. Poets need care little if they be called obscure by Philistines.' "[3] Nevertheless, much of Wheelwright's poetry is so difficult that even the most sympathetic reader may well end up feeling that, if this is difficulty, please pass the obscurity.

Why then bother with Wheelwright at all? A good question, and one for which I hope to come up with an answer before I have done. I suppose one answer might be something akin to W. S. Gilbert's "If this young man expresses himself in terms too deep for *me* / Why, what a very singularly deep young

man this deep young man must be!"[4] Except that in Wheel-
wright's case, one can say it without satire. Even where I can-
not finally grasp his meaning, which is much of the time, I
remain convinced by the extraordinary power of his lan-
guage as it flashes by on its way from somewhere to some-
where else. At times it seems like higher mathematics; I can
sense the "elegance" of his solutions without being able to
follow the steps by which he arrives at them. In short, he is a
poet from whom one takes a great deal on faith, but one does
it voluntarily. His conviction is contagious.

Wheelwright was born on September 9, 1897, in Milton,
Massachusetts, to a distinguished New England family. His
father, Edmund March Wheelwright, was a noted architect
who served for several years as official architect to the city of
Boston. Among his designs are the New England Conserva-
tory of Music, Horticultural Hall, and the Longfellow
Bridge. His last completed building was the eccentrically pic-
turesque Lampoon Building in 1909; he had been a co-
founder of the magazine while a Harvard undergraduate. He
was the ninth direct descendant of the Reverend John Wheel-
wright of Cambridge University, kinsman of John Dryden,
who emigrated to Massachusetts in 1636. In the Antinomian
Controversy, this ancestor supported his sister-in-law, Anne
Hutchinson, and was condemned for sedition and contro-
versy. Banished from Boston, he founded Exeter, New
Hampshire, and later the outpost town of Wells, Maine. His
descendant John Wheelwright the poet always felt close to
his ancestor; in his poem "Bread-Word Giver," he addresses
him as "John, founder of towns—dweller in none; / Wheel-

wright, schismatic,—schismatic from schismatics; / friend of great men whom these great feared greatly; / Saint, whose name and business I bear with me; / rebel New England's rebel against dominion."[5]

John Wheelwright's mother, Elizabeth Brooks, was the great-granddaughter of Peter Chardon Brooks, in his day the wealthiest merchant in New England; and both sides of the family were connected to a number of other prominent New England families. Jack, as he was called, was one of three children, including a sister, Louise, who would later marry Jack's friend S. Foster Damon, the Blake scholar and poet, and an older brother, March. Much of his childhood was spent on a vast estate at Medford that had belonged to his great-great grandfather, which during Jack's lifetime was sold to developers and built over as Boston expanded. Jack called it, in words that typically reflect his pride in his aristocratic heritage and his radical political conscience: "the most splendid garden of Massachusetts . . . Even as it was built of profits from the exploitation of the sea, so it has long been destroyed by profit-seeking exploitation of the land. The fact that its fate was its appropriate destiny gives no comfort to them who loved it, and who, with its vanishing, found themselves deprived, as by a racial blood-letting, of the body of their cultural heritage."[6]

The family lived part of the time in Europe during Jack's childhood, and he later attended St. George's School in Newport, Rhode Island. In 1912, while he was still a student there, the first of a series of tragedies occurred that began the family's slow decline into genteel poverty: his father committed suicide. Another setback came in 1920 when Jack was expelled from Harvard during his last year for a series of anti-authoritarian pranks.

Wheelwright had begun writing poems while still a student at St. George's and continued to do so at Harvard; later, many of these juvenilia would be published or incorporated in other poems, as he had the habit of constantly working and reworking them. After the appearance of *Eight More Harvard Poets,* he spent two years in Florence, where his family had rented a villa, and there published as a pamphlet in 1924 a long poem called "North Atlantic Passage." While in Europe, he also worked as an editor with Malcolm Cowley and Matthew Josephson on the magazine *Secession,* which Gorham Munson had founded in Vienna. Munson eventually quarreled with all of them and particularly castigated Wheelwright for publishing a mangled version of Hart Crane's "For the Marriage of Faustus and Helen." Jack eventually apologized for this to Crane, who generously forgave him; the incident is alluded to in a poem called "Fish Food, An Obituary to Hart Crane." This was one of several long poems collected amid shorter lyrics in Wheelwright's first volume, *Rock and Shell,* which he had printed in 1933 by a small Boston publisher, Bruce Humphries. With "North Atlantic Passage," these poems chart a religious odyssey that had begun with his abandonment of Unitarianism, which he came to consider "a debased form of religion . . . [that] 'had freed the Brahmins from the fear of damnation, so the Brahmins supposed that they themselves were saved,'"[7] for Anglo-Catholicism and eventually socialism. "Forty Days" deals with "the season which falls between Christ's rising

from the grave and his mounting from the earth." One
source was the New Testament Apocrypha presented in Rev-
erend Sabine Baring-Gould's "Lost and Hostile Gospels";
in his note to the poem, Wheelwright, disposed by his lin-
eage to heresy, states: "Many uncanonical sayings of Jesus
preserved by the Fathers' refutation of false constructions
long put upon them, are consistent with Gospel sayings; and
this uncanonical wisdom, in the author's ear, recovers for
systematic Christianity moral qualities which Quietists now
leave to Sceptics."[8] Another major poem is "Twilight,"
based largely on the apocryphal Acts of Thomas, the doubt-
ing apostle who was Wheelwright's favorite saint. Still others
are "To Wise Men on the Death of a Fool," another elegy,
this one for the Lost Generation bohemian Harry Crosby;
and "Come Over and Help Us," which Wheelwright says
"embodies in part the author's response to the case of Sacco
and Vanzetti during the latter year of whose trial it was
composed."[9]

Throughout the 1920s, Jack had managed to live and
dress like a dandy on an allowance of fifteen hundred dollars
a year; his lodgings consisted of a railroad flat on Marlbor-
ough Street. In the 1930s the family's sinking fortunes,
caused in part by his brother's business reversals, wiped out
even that income, and Jack moved back to his mother's
house on Beacon Street. He joined the Socialist Party in
1932; when it split in 1936, he went with the Trotskyites and
became active in the Socialist Workers Party, embarking on a
round of political activity which included giving street-
corner addresses to workers (sometimes attired in his signa-
ture raccoon coat) and helping found the John Reed Society

at Harvard and the spinoff Rebel Arts Society. He initiated a correspondence course aimed at formulating a proletarian poetry, called "The Form and Content of Rebel Poetry." He published an occasional little magazine called *Poems for a Dime;* longer issues were entitled *Poems for Two Bits.* Through it all, he still clung, almost until the end of his life, to his own brand of Marxist Christianity, which frequently involved him in disputes with his more orthodox leftist colleagues. As Alvin Rosenfeld has said, "In the end, his political quarrels, which he often carried out on the level of speculative theology, isolated him from the mainstream of Socialism, and he seems to have finally stood alone as something of a one-man party."[10]

Rock and Shell was followed in 1938 by *Mirrors of Venus, A Novel in Sonnets,* also printed by Bruce Humphries in an edition of five hundred copies. The title is taken from a painting by Sir Edward Burne-Jones, wherein, Wheelwright says, "the mirror of Venus reflects loved ones as each would be seen."[11] It is a dazzling series of sonnets, some orthodox, some bizarre, some recent and others dating from his adolescence, whose theme is the loss of friendship and a philosophic coming to terms with it. In contrast, *Political Self-Portrait* of 1940, the last volume of Wheelwright's poetry to appear during his lifetime, moves away from the personal to the political, at any rate to Wheelwright's unorthodox poetic assimilation of it. Shortly after it was published, Wheelwright was run over and killed by a drunken driver, on September 15, 1940, less than a week after his forty-third birthday and at the height of his creative powers. Tragically, with the new volume he had seemed at last poised for recognition as one of the leading American poets of his time.

In the following year, 1941, New Directions brought out a slim *Selected Poems* including unpublished work as well as poems from the previous collections, with an introduction by R. P. Blackmur. The jacket copy stated that "a complete edition of Wheelwright's poetry is in preparation but it will not be ready for a year or more."[12] This proved to be an understatement, since the *Collected Poems* wasn't brought out by New Directions until 1972, shortly after the death of S. Foster Damon, Wheelwright's brother-in-law and literary executor. By this time Wheelwright was all but totally forgotten, except for occasional critical essays, chiefly those of Alvin H. Rosenfeld, who edited the *Collected Poems* and was at one time said to be at work on a biography of the poet, and Alan Wald, whose 1983 book *The Revolutionary Imagination,* which discusses chiefly from a political point of view the poetry of Wheelwright and that of his college friend and fellow Marxist Sherry Mangan, is the most substantial critical study of him to date. Possibly this is one result of a recent resurgence of Marxism in literary academia. In any case, it is something to be grateful for, since Wald is attentive not only to Wheelwright's ideologies but to his prosody as well and is invaluable at decoding some of the knottier "arguments," to use Wheelwright's own term, that underlie the poems and are essential for coming to terms with them. Still, full-length critical and biographical studies of this *poète maudit* are sorely needed.

At the center of everything Wheelwright wrote, and at the core of his being insofar as we can know it from his own

testimony and that of those who knew him, is a contradic-
tion, a cleavage that corresponds to the Cubist impulse I
mentioned in connection with Roussel: the unsatisfiable but
imperious urge to see all sides of an object, which turns up
wherever we look in modernism—not just in the work of the
Cubists themselves but in the flattening process that goes on
in serial music, in the inextricable linking of fabulous past
and mundane present in James Joyce's *Ulysses;* in the all-
seeing eye of Proust's narrator; in the erasures of Willem de
Kooning, where the viewer must make his own difficult, if
not impossible, transitions in order to construe the image
being offered for consideration. Wheelwright's inborn ten-
dency to elide transitions is what makes his writing at once
so exciting and so problematical; indeed, these two aspects
of his writing tend to merge wherever one looks. It is for him
not so much the ability to see both sides of any given issue,
but the inability not to. True, much of this is a conscious tac-
tic, as he states in a short essay on poetic craft first published
by Alvin Rosenfeld in 1972:

Idealogical [*sic*] music is closely related to dissociation of associ-
ated ideas and the association of the disassociated. This philo-
sophical process must constantly go on, in answer to constantly
changing society, for ages and generations and for individuals
from childhood to old age and from mood to mood. This makes
spirits athletic, not only to guard against change, but to wel-
come change. The poetry keeps you awake. If it makes you
dream, it warns you that you are half-asleep. Its magic is not
hypnosis but frenzy . . . Its wisdom is not the philosophical love
of wisdom but the psychological knowledge of the soul.[13]

Yet even when writing straightforward critical prose, Wheelwright cannot resist the urge to leap from an idea to its opposite without transition. In a review of Robert Frost's *A Further Range,* he has some harsh things to say about the older poet: "Frost's good work is beyond his audience. His other work is beneath them. As [Edwin Arlington] Robinson was a favorite with Theodore Roosevelt, Frost at his worst is a poetic Calvin Coolidge for the Herbert Hoovers . . . His Conservatism vs. Radicalism is a half-toasted substitute for half-baked bread." But in his final paragraph, Wheelwright abruptly shifts gears: "He holds his own because he is distinct among all his rivals and because a teeming welter of talent, finer in prosody and firmer in philosophy, is so indistinct by reason of keen rivalry that no critic has picked any one poet to match against Robert Frost."[14] And in another book review, this one of Muriel Rukeyser, he offers in the same paragraph his recipe for poetry for the masses in two difficult-to-reconcile dicta: "One political use of poetry is to single out the body of the elect," and "Revolutionary writing in the snob style does not reach a proper audience."[15]

In person as well as in his writing, Wheelwright was literally a set of walking contradictions. Matthew Josephson describes him as "a thin, long-legged blond youth with pale blue eyes and a long nose. He would always appear in tight-fitting, sharply creased suits, a bowler and carrying a Malacca cane, even when we all set off for a walk in the country clad in comfortable old clothes. He traveled about Europe, moreover, with fully fourteen pairs of shoes, every inch of him the dandy nonconformist; and held forth both as a social rebel and devoutly religious Anglican."[16] Still another paradox in Wheelwright's character which has been mentioned but not much discussed, perhaps because of a dearth of documentation, was his ambiguous sexuality. Alan Wald mentions an "unpublished journal Jack kept during his period of residence in Italy" (1922–1924, now in his papers at Brown University), which not only "shows a surprising openness to the fascist political movement of Mussolini" but also "chronicles adventures in whorehouses and hints at homosexual experiments."[17] True, but since the journal in question was obviously kept for himself alone, Jack was hinting to himself—rather an odd thing to do. And his visit to at least one Florentine brothel was strictly as a voyeur. While describing with relish the various sex acts staged for his benefit, he says he declined politely whenever invited to join in. Afterward he notes that though the experience cost him twenty dollars, it was worth twenty thousand, and concludes with the self-exhortation, "Try everything once." Yet, on this occasion at any rate, he had tried nothing; participation meant merely observing.

The incident is worth noting because Wheelwright hints at a homosexual aspect to the many-sided but nominally platonic friendship that is the pretext of *Mirrors of Venus,* though it is by no means the only subject. One of the sonnets is bluntly entitled "Phallus," and begins with the lines "Friends need not guard each other as a jealous / Moslem must segregate his odalisque, / no more than one need see the symboled phallus / while meditating at an obelisk." True enough, but then why bother to bring it up? Yet the final couplet seems to hint at repression: "Habit is evil—all habit, even speech; / and promises prefigure their own breach."[18] In another sonnet in the series, "Sophomore," he ends: "He preferred / talk with autumnal women, ever mellow, / or boys, with whom his well-considered word / not always marked him as a crazy fellow."[19] An earlier version of this poem in a notebook has Wheelwright speaking in the first rather than the third person.

Yet, although he condemns as a sin sexual abstinence in a married couple in the poem "Twilight," which deals with the apocryphal adventures of St. Thomas, one can easily imagine Jack recoiling from sex, both with boys and with mellow women. Josephson describes a conversation during which Jack wept while describing a presumably homosexual act that had taken place at boarding school years before; would not such a feeling of guilt also inhibit his conduct as an adult? Yet some evidence seems to indicate that he felt similarly repressed with women. Two poems in *Rock and Shell*, "Slow Curtain" and "Quick Curtain," both dedicated to Mary Opdycke Pelz, describe a kiss that fails to materialize as the curtain falls on a play. The first ends with the lines: "The piece comes to an end. The lovers face one another. Neither moves a muscle. / There is no applause";[20] the second with the line, "We had grown wise in all things before love."[21] The painter Fairfield Porter, who was a friend of Wheelwright's during their Trotskyist days, told me that Jack's frequent crushes on women never seemed to pan out, that they seldom found him attractive; yet photographs show him to have been a striking, even romantic-looking figure. Still another anecdote concerns an engagement party in New York where he danced all evening with his intended; a few days later, friends found that the lady had broken the engagement off.

These circumstances seem worth mentioning because they round out the cluster of contradictions from which his work emerges: the repeated stretching toward opposite poles wherein he stops just short of closure, whether from timidity or from too much wisdom: he had grown wise in all things before love. I tend to suspect the latter because of the positive results of failure in his work. It isn't a question of Eliot's "shadow" that falls between the conception and the act, but a fertile short-circuiting, the result of many tensions pulling in opposite directions, that is the air his poetry breathes. Rather than chaos, the resulting layers of ambiguity result in a dense transparency. I'd like now to look at one of Wheelwright's most beautiful and seemingly straightforward lyrics to illustrate how dense this clarity can get. It's called "Why Must You Know?" and is in the form of a dialogue between two speakers, although in the inevitable complicating footnote he tells us that they may be voices of the same mind or of different persons:

> —"What was that sound we heard
> fall on the snow?"
> —"It was a frozen bird.
> Why must you know?
> All the dull earth knows the good
> that the air, with claws and wings
> tears to the scattered questionings
> which burn in fires of our blood."

—"Let the air's beak and claws
    carry my deeds
far, where no springtime thaws
    the frost for their seeds."
—"One could fathom every sound
that the circling blood can tell
who heard the diurnal syllable,
while lying close against the ground."
—"My flesh, bone and sinew
    now would discern
hidden waters in you
    Earth, waters that burn."
—"One who turns to earth again
finds solace in its weight; and deep
hears the blood forever keep
the silence between drops of rain."[22]

Something is slightly askew even in the first couplet: "What was that sound we heard / fall on the snow?" It wasn't the sound that fell on the snow, but the frozen bird that produced the sound, as the next line makes clear. Still, this opening gambit is typical of Wheelwright's fondness for toying with the reader by keeping even his most straightforward proclamations slightly off balance. After answering the question, the second speaker demands, "Why must you know?" But it isn't a question of trying to shut out the horrid knowledge of nature red in tooth and claw, as at first seems to be the case: "All the dull earth knows the good / that the air, with claws and wings / tears to the scattered questionings / which burn in fires of our blood." The beak and claws are capable of something more positive than death, since the scattered questionings will burn in fires of our blood and presumably keep us warm and alive. Yet the first speaker would forgo this benefit, preferring that the air's beak and claws transport him to a place of frozen inactivity, where spring cannot thaw the frost that keeps seeds dormant. The first speaker, meanwhile, goes on either to change the subject or to annotate it cryptically by stating that every sound that the circling blood can tell can be heard simply by listening to the single diurnal syllable which is audible to one who lies close against the ground. This announcement inspires the first speaker to now wish to discern in earth "hidden waters that burn," an elixir, apparently, that will both satisfy thirst and supply life-promoting warmth. And the second speaker seems to agree, albeit obliquely, by stating that one who turns to earth again, Antaeus-like, finds solace in its weight—a relief, apparently, from the weightless air with its claws, beak, and wings that can accomplish both good and evil— and can experience the advantage in hearing the blood, which is in the earth, forever keep the silence between drops of rain, which descend from the air unharmed (as the frozen bird did not), ready to thaw the seeds that the other speaker originally wanted to stay frozen. Thus the poem seems to be a highly circuitous return from the contemplation of death to the possibility of embracing life, a kind of *valse hésitation* whose rhythms recall what we know of Wheelwright's affective life.

To illustrate what I meant by calling this poem comparatively accessible, here is another short lyric in the same vein, though infinitely more recalcitrant while even more resonant with potential meanings.

> Any Friend to Any Friend
> $$(A - B)^2 = (B - A)^2$$
>
> On outskirts of the woods of thought
> B saw A bow his head
> to mourn the death of one B sought . . .
>   and found himself was dead.
>
> A dug one grave for corpse and man.
>   And turned aside to laugh.
> But when B rose to dig, A ran
>   upon B with the staff,
>
> which B had cut A when it leaved
>   (though it ran blood, not sap)
> There was no combat. They both grieved,
>   fallen, across the dead man's lap.[23]

I shall not attempt an exegesis, beyond observing that the equation with its squares seems to suggest a deprivation of friendship that is squared by the magnified importance one friend takes on in the habitat of another's mind; and that the two characters named A and B with the third unnamed dead one might suggest the legend of Cain and Abel, a recurring theme in Wheelwright, one of whose alter egos, along with doubting Thomas, was Seth, the third son of Adam and Eve.

The sonnets of *Mirrors of Venus* are frequently less demanding and tense than these early ones, yet their shifts of tone can be just as bewildering. The first in the series, a lament for a friend named Ned Couch, who was killed in an accident at Fort Leavenworth at the beginning of World War I, begins in a disarmingly folksy tone that could be out of the *Saturday Evening Post*:

> Perhaps a lot of you have lost a friend,—
> a friend who had a way of saying things
> you can't remember, yet you can't forget,—
> things which make you almost weep for more
> now that you know that more can never come,—

So far so good, but the octave ends: "A friend not made to die till the chrysalis / of sense peeled from him and his sixth sense learned / it had been born to supra-sensual moths." Here is the concluding octave, which makes sixteen lines. (Other sonnets in the sequence have seven, thirteen, or fifteen lines.)

> Out there at Leavenworth that bored you;
> shy at your shoulder-strap; back among friends;
> and then Across;—"An overdose of morphine"?
> That is absurd. Mere doctors could not kill
> a soldier who detested war, a soldier
> thus self-inoculated against death.
> > Ned. Ned.
> Why, after twenty years, do I think you killed
> > yourself?[24]

Thus one theme of the sonnet sequence, Ned's tragically
early death perhaps by suicide, is announced, but matters by
no means end there. For Wheelwright's father, the architect,
was also named Ned and killed himself. This memory
inspires one of Wheelwright's most poignant and direct ut-
terances, strangely anticipatory of Robert Lowell, as Wheel-
wright contemplates the "bridge of turrets" his father built,
the one the subway crosses from Boston to Cambridge, at-
tacked by sulphurous pollution while neon signs dwarf the
authority of the statehouse dome. The sestet is a passionate,
almost hopeful invitation to his father, "first friend" who
"made your mind my home," an allusion both to that mind
and to the building that issued from it.

> Father
>
> An East Wind asperges Boston with Lynn's sulphurous
>   brine.
> Under the bridge of turrets my father built,—from
>   turning sign
> Of CHEVROLET, out-topping our gilt State House
>   dome
> to burning sign of CARTER'S INK,—drip multitudes
> of checker-board shadows. Inverted turreted
>   reflections
> sleeting over axle-grease billows, through all
>   directions
> cross-cut parliamentary gulls, who toss like gourds.
>
> Speak. Speak to me again, as fresh saddle leather
>   (Speak; talk again) to a hunter smells of heather.

> Come home. Wire a wire of warning without
> words.
> Come home and talk to me again, my first friend.
> Father,
> come home, dead man, who made your mind my
> home.[25]

And as Alan Wald points out, there is yet a third Ned involved in the sequence: "Ned" Burne-Jones, whose painting provides the title of the series of sonnets, *Mirrors of Venus*.[26] Just to complicate things further, the central character, whose estrangement provided Wheelwright with the text for his discursive sermon on the frailty of human relationships, is a non-Ned named Richardson King Wood.

I have spoken of some of Wheelwright's shorter, comparatively lyrical poems, even though the soul of his poetry is in the series of longer ones, radically experimental in form and quite as pregnant with options for the future of poetry as anything that Pound or Eliot produced. But as is evident from the short poems just cited, their density and complexity are such that even to attempt a cursory description of them would be far beyond the scope of this introduction to Wheelwright's work. Still, it is instructive to note some of their characteristics, and I shall try to do so, choosing an early and a late example.

"North Atlantic Passage," written apparently during Wheelwright's ocean crossing to Europe in 1922, alternates prose evocations of the churning surface of the ocean with brief connecting passages of verse, some of it rhymed; Wald suggests Amy Lowell's "Can Grande's Castle" as a possible antecedent,[27] and John Gould Fletcher's color symphonies might well be another, but the medium Wheelwright uses is far more radical and original than either of these tentative attempts at modernism.

As usual, Wheelwright's "Argument" is of little help in deciphering the poem. Here it is, however, for what it is worth:

Man, looking at the World as form in motion, sees the enigma of the One and the Many reflected on the mirror of the past. In his desire for future security he seeks to learn from fancy and imagination the nature, if not the answer, of the enigma. But all he learns from studying the past is that facts do not fuse with truth. He learns neither the cause nor the degree of this antipathy, for the enigma clouds the mirror.

Man gives himself up to enjoying the distractions of the present show. But the paradox appears that he is part of what he sees. Dissolved into the external world, he becomes an enigma to himself. It is then that he turns towards Authority to bring him assurance.

But again fact, whether seen as Being or as Becoming, proves a foundation insufficient for the authoritative superstructure. The Reason, worn by relentless flux, fears lest it dissolve away, and leaves outer facts of sense for inner truths of thought to find Authority.

Man, shut from the outside world, is shut from the enigma. But the counter paradox appears and remains, though reason and the five senses fade: it is only upon his own internal Authority that he can accept external Authority. The soul had almost become the One, but the Many breaks through its barriers and order comes to an end. Yet Man rebels against disorder. The

Reason and Memory help him only a little. But, though the senses are worn, he gathers his forces; and turned from the past, goes seeking to find that immediate and present assurance which is required.[28]

From there, Wheelwright plunges us directly into the sea. Here he pictures beautifully the sea's chaos, as he does also in a further section where he speaks of whitecaps that are "climbing never, always mounting / slipping always, never sinking."[29] But we soon find that an imagistic painting of the sea isn't what he intends: after the words "foam fallen on spray," he describes the black marble pavements as "clustered like bullets / bullets in embryo, clust'ring round a cold bullet mould"[30]—already description is starting to pull away from the object described to enter a synthesizing phase that becomes increasingly chaotic, as he introduces "the distractions of the present show":

A wind like a razor shaves the lather from my whiskers. Across the floor of ashen and black marble, the hem-stitched and shirred ruching and ruffles; starched petticoats, under-and-over skirts of ball dresses, with scarves, capes, tippets, shawls, boas, and opera cloaks; all together now,—lash rush and tumble.— Flopping and swishing, frowsy, sloppy chic; sweeping swerving fan and sword dancers; Benjamin Franklin's incandescent Daughters strike attitudes of various hysteria before the zenith of Catherine the Great's umbrageous Sons. The Dance of form and light swaps with the Dance of shadow and color. In the bald-headed row, Barbarossa slumbers on the lap of Prester John,—while the budding Blossom bursts apart; its petals uncurl in acanthine grace; and the Lotus lolls serenely on the Waters.[31]

Noting that "Christians, to please the Mother of God / call her the Star of the Sea," he next plunges us into a whirlpool of Christian and pagan symbols pitted against and ultimately annihilating one another. In his footnote to the poem, Wheelwright acknowledges various sources for his collage, including "an anonymous exclamation made at the Jamestown [presumably Johnstown] flood"; that ejaculation is "To the hills for your lives! The dam has burst!" and it precipitates the debacle when "the Many breaks through its barriers" and order comes to an end. But at the very last, as promised, "Man gathers his forces; and turned from the past, goes seeking to find that immediate and present assurance which is required," and the poem ends where it began: "Lead us from opalescent / rainbows, through rainbows / to black opal."[32]

In a notebook entry on the poem, Wheelwright described his method of composition: "After gazing at the ocean for several days, phrases formed themselves in my mind and were repeated so insistently by the sound of the engines and the ocean that I was compelled to write them down. . . . My method throughout appears to have been that which has subsequently been made known to the world under the name *sur-realism*."[33] But on reflecting, he concluded that it "was a good example of a bad thing." "Had the *sur-realist* method led me . . . to put down everything except precisely what I was saying?"

Further reflections on form from the same unpublished Italian notebook prompted these observations: "Choose one's audience as carefully as one does one's enemies. In a landscape how most trees or pieces of rock or water might all as well be somewhere else. I speak of nature not of paint. That now and again there is a tree or rock or water which exists from all sides, does not look well from this hedge or that gate only but casts radiance and magnetism all about it, making everything as far as the horizon different for its presence. That is the only art worth bothering with. Not art that adorns and softens life but art which is at once a benediction and a judgment."

It was in the last, great poems of *Political Self-Portrait* and the posthumous collection *Dusk to Dusk* that Wheelwright was finally able to achieve this end: "art which is at once a benediction and a judgment." The problem of art by the one for the many, of singling out an elite audience by addressing mankind in general, finally triumphed over the contradictions with which Wheelwright wrestled in works like the ebullient but chaotic soup of "North Atlantic Passage." To this latter group belong major long poems like "Twilight," "The Dark before the Day," and particularly "Train Ride," to my mind his greatest poem, in which he rings the changes on a Marxist slogan attributed to the German socialist Karl Liebknecht: "Always the enemy is the foe at home," until it resonates with many meanings.[34] The call to social action is still dominant, but amplified as a call to all human action, very much in the manner of the contemporary composer Frederic Rzewski's magnificent set of variations (1975) on the Chilean workers' chant known in North America as "The People United Will Never Be Defeated":

Train Ride

FOR HORACE GREGORY

After rain, through afterglow, the unfolding fan
of railway landscape sidled on the pivot

of a larger arc into the green of evening;
I remembered that noon I saw a gradual bud
still white; though dead in its warm bloom;
always the enemy is the foe at home.

And I wondered what surgery could recover
our lost, long stride of indolence and leisure
which is labor in reverse; what physic recall the
    smile
not of lips, but of eyes as of the sea bemused.

We, when we disperse from common sleep to
        several
tasks, we gather to despair; we, who assembled
once for hopes from common toil to dreams
or sickish and hurting or triumphal rapture;
always our enemy is our foe at home.

We, deafened with far scattered city rattles
to the hubbub of forest birds (never having
"had time" to grieve or to hear through vivid sleep
the sea knock on its cracked and hollow stones)
so that the stars, almost, and birds comply,
and the garden-wet; the trees retire; We are
a scared patrol, fearing the guns behind;
always the enemy is the foe at home.

What wonder that we fear our own eyes' look
and fidget to be at home alone, and pitifully
put off age by some change in brushing the hair
and stumble to our ends like smothered runners at
    their tape;

We follow our shreds of fame into an ambush.

    Then (as while the stars herd to the great trough
the blind, in the always-only-outward of their
   dismantled
archways, awake at the smell of warmed stone
or to the sound of reeds, lifting from the dim
into their segment of green dawn) *always
our enemy is our foe at home,* more
certainly than through spoken words or from grief-
twisted writing on paper, unblotted by tears
the thought came:
                There is no physic
for the world's ill, nor surgery; it must
(hot smell of tar on wet salt air)
burn in a fever forever, an incense pierced
with arrows, whose name is Love and another name
Rebellion (the twinge, the gulf, split seconds,
the very raindrop, render, and instancy
of Love).
    All Poetry to this not-to-be-looked-upon sun
of Passion is the moon's cupped light; all
Politics to this moon, a moon's reflected
cupped light, like the moon of Rome, after
the deep wells of Grecian light sank low;
always the enemy is the foe at home.
    But these three are friends whose arms twine
without words; as, in a still air,
the great grove leans to wind, past and to come.[35]

V

▲ "The Unthronged Oracle"

Laura Riding

In looking back at the poets I have discussed so far, I find
that each of them requires some kind of special handling.
That is, reading their work isn't quite as simple as it is
with a poet such as, say, John Keats, where one can simply
take down a book from a shelf, open it, and begin reading
and enjoying it. With each of them, some previous adjust-
ment or tuning is required. It also helps to know some-
thing of their biographies and the circumstances in which
they worked, since these are responsible for wide fluctua-
tions in the quality of what they wrote. With Clare, for
example, it helps to know that extreme poverty forced
him to turn out potboilers for the well-paying literary
annuals, and that poverty was a factor in the insanity that
caused him to spend the last three decades of his life in
a madhouse, where the nature of his illness and possibly
the well-meaning corrections of a scribe resulted in poetry
that varies from the sublime to the wretched. With Bed-
does, one has to look for poetry embedded in impossible
plays, closet dramas that refuse to stay in the closet but
have nowhere else to go. Nor can Beddoes's best poetry
be easily extricated from them; except for some songs
and isolated purple passages, it is intricately woven

into the dramatic fabric. In the case of Roussel, the facts of his life play such an infinitesimal role that one is again forced to readjust one's preconceived notions of what writing is; here it is so unlike daily reality as to seem a separate planet, with its own laws of gravity and duration. Wheelwright provides his own critical apparatus in the form of notes and arguments that jostle the poetry's claim on the reader's attention. While it is possible to take the poetry straight, it isn't quite the same as it is when considered simultaneously with the author's frequently unilluminating commentaries: it seems to gain something from the proximity of that foil, even when the apparatus is nothing more than a foil. I don't know what it says about my own poetry that I like these poets: whether it means that I too wish to be given "special treatment," or that for some reason I like writing that isn't simple, where there is more than at first meets the eye—or both. I bring up the point because, as I mentioned in the first chapter, I chose the writers under discussion partly because I like them and partly because I felt they would shed some light on my own writing for those who feel the need of it. So far, I agree, not much of the latter has happened, but perhaps by the end it will have, if only by default.

Laura Riding is a writer whose work demands more attention and attentiveness than any of those discussed so far. Before showing why this is, I shall endeavor to dispose of the relevant biographical facts as quickly as possible. She was born in Brooklyn in 1901 to nonreligious Jewish parents named Reichenthal; her father, a tailor, was a fervent socialist who had hopes that his daughter might grow up to be an

American Rosa Luxemburg; however, she retained a lifelong disdain for politics, particularly of the left. In 1922, she married a professor of English named Louis Gottschalk, and her first poems were published under the name Laura Riding Gottschalk. She has said that she considered the name Laura Reichenthal Gottschalk too cumbersome; I have never been able to find out why she chose the name Riding. In any event, she seems to have had a fondness for pseudonyms; at various times she used the names Madeleine Vary, Lilith Outcome, and Barbara Rich. She disowned the last name, but Robert Graves says she used it for a book they wrote together called *No Decency Left,* of which I have been unable to find a copy. (It should be noted that many of her books were published in tiny editions, and most are today extremely difficult to locate.) After her marriage in 1941 to the writer Schuyler Jackson, she used the name Laura (Riding) Jackson.

The Gottschalks were divorced in 1925. After a year in New York, where she frequented bohemian literary circles and became friendly with Hart Crane, Riding moved to England at the suggestion of Robert Graves, who had seen and admired her poetry in the Nashville literary review, *The Fugitive,* to which Graves too contributed. Although she never lived in Nashville, she became closely associated with the group, which included Allen Tate, John Crowe Ransom, Robert Penn Warren, Merrill Moore, and Donald Davidson; from August 1923 until the magazine's demise in December 1925, her poetry appeared in every issue. Riding had not met Graves before moving to London, but she immediately became part of the Graves ménage there, an arrangement that seemed to suit everyone, including Graves's wife, Nancy

Nicholson, who sometimes lived on a houseboat in the Thames with their four children. (Riding tried to suppress most biographical information relating to herself; for what is given here, I am indebted to Joyce Piell Wexler's 1980 critical study, *Laura Riding's Pursuit of Truth,* and to secondary sources cited by her.)[1]

Riding's first book of poems, *The Close Chaplet,* was published by Leonard and Virginia Woolf's Hogarth Press in 1926; the title comes from a line of Graves's: "the close chaplet of thought";[2] the book is dedicated to Riding's sister, Isabel, and to Graves's wife, Nancy. In 1927, Graves and Riding bought a hand press and founded the Seizin Press, whose name comes from a legal term meaning freehold possession, and they began to publish books of which they approved, including their own. As Graves put it, "We were our own masters and no longer dependent on publishers who would tell us that our poems did not fit the image of poetry which they wished to present to the public."[3] All seemed to go smoothly until the arrival on the scene early in 1929 of an Irish poet named Geoffrey Phibbs, which further complicated a ménage already complicated even by Bloomsbury standards. The eventual disastrous result was that Laura leapt from a third-story window, not to commit suicide but to break the spell, as she said, which bound her to the three persons in the room at the time: Robert, Nancy, and Phibbs. Her spine was broken in several places, and she endured months of agonizing convalescence tended by Graves; meanwhile, his wife went off to live with Phibbs, who eventually changed his name to Taylor. Graves and Riding moved themselves and the Seizin Press to the village of

Deyá, Mallorca, which Gertrude Stein had recommended as a cheap and agreeable place to live; they were to remain there until the Spanish Civil War forced them to leave in 1936.

The Deyá years, where Riding seemed to undergo a resurrection after the death-haunted poetry that had preceded her leap, were the most productive of her life. Her two masterpieces of prose fiction, *Progress of Stories* and *Lives of Wives*, date from then, as does *A Trojan Ending*, a witty novel about the Trojan War. *Everybody's Letters*, a wonderfully entertaining collection of mundane letters by everybody and anybody, which shows Riding at her funniest even though she claimed not to have written any of them, also dates from that period. The bulk of the poetry assembled in the 1938 *Collected Poems* was written in Deyá. There were as well other collections of short prose fictions and/or criticism, and an ambitious occasional periodical called *Epilogue*, designed, in Joyce Wexler's words, "to present her discoveries of truth to an audience her poetry did not reach."[4]

All this feverish activity ended abruptly when the war forced the exiles of Deyá to leave almost at a moment's notice, with only a suitcase apiece, abandoning the printing press as well as many manuscripts and documents. After brief stays in London, Paris, and Switzerland, Graves, Riding, and a small group of disciples came to America in the spring of 1939, settling in New Hope, Pennsylvania. Shortly afterward, a new and definitive recombining of relationships occurred. A friend introduced Laura to a charismatic writer named Schuyler Jackson, who had written a glowing review of her *Collected Poems* for *Time* magazine, where he worked as poetry editor, a post which apparently no longer exists.

The two fell in love, while another couple who were part of the group, Alan and Beryl Hodge, got divorced. Graves left for England, where he eventually married Mrs. Hodge. Riding and Jackson were married in 1941 and moved to a village in northern Florida called Wabasso, where Riding lived until her death in 1991. They made a living at citrus growing; their aim, evidently, was to isolate themselves as completely as possible from the world of letters in order to discover "truth." This led to Riding's renunciation of poetry and to their collaboration on what she was later to define as "a work on language in which the relation between the spiritual basis of language and the rational principles informing it is traced, and the operation of those principles explored in the patternings of word-meaning; the work's object is the demonstration of the dependence of good (in all the senses) diction on the use of words with attentive regard for their individual rational nature, and the general function of language as the articulation of our humanness." The title of this work was to be "Rational Meaning: A New Foundation for the Definition of Words."[5]

Poet: A Lying Word had been the title of a collection of Riding's poetry and prose published in 1933; she now began to live the conditions implied in that title, writing no new poetry or fiction and refusing to allow her early work to be reprinted, at least until 1964, when she gave me permission to reprint the story "A Last Lesson in Geography" in the review *Art and Literature,* of which I was an editor. In 1970, two years after Schuyler Jackson's death, she authorized Faber and Faber to reprint a small *Selected Poems* with an introduction in which she warned readers not to construe these poems as poetry in the generally understood sense of the term. She justified her decision to allow the reprinting of them as follows:

There will be reading of the poems in this book without reference to the preface, and with my consciousness of this goes an inconsistency in co-operating in making them available, since it is not my interest merely to add to the quantity of easily available poetic reading-matter. I judge my poems to be things of the first water as poetry, but that does not make them better than poetry, and I think poetry obstructs general attainment to something better in our linguistic way-of-life than we have. I can only hope that the poems themselves will soften this inconsistency by making the nature of poetry, to which they are faithful, plainer, in its forced, fine suspension of truth; poetry and truth have been so much hashed that there is little whole perception of what they are.[6]

She went on to expand her views of the difference between truth and poetry at great and some would say tedious length in a "personal evangel" called *The Telling*.[7]

As may be evident from what I have said so far, Laura Riding was what we would call today a "control freak." Her poetry, hedged about with caveats of every sort in the form of admonitory prefaces and postscripts, presents us with something like a minefield; one reads it always with a sensation of sirens and flashing red lights in the background. What then are we to do with a body of poetry whose author warns us that we have very little chance of understanding it, and who believes that poetry itself is a lie? Why, misread it, of course, if it seems to merit reading, as hers so obviously does. This is what happens to any poetry: no poem can ever hope to produce the exact sensation in even one reader that the poet intended; all poetry is written with this understanding on the part of poet and reader; if it can't stand the test of what Harold Bloom names "misprision," then we leave it to pass on to something else. Fortunately, Riding's poetry does pass the test, even though this is the last thing she would have wanted.

There is something truly touching in Laura Riding's extraordinary attempt to control the way her poetry is read, because it is such an extreme example of what every poet would like to arrange for his or her own work. One factor in it is no doubt an exaggerated aversion to evaluation, which all of us have to some degree. If the poet can convince us we are incapable of reading her correctly, then there will be no question of our being able to tell her good poems from her bad ones; all will exist on a plane remote from us where such differences in degree do not even exist. And Riding's intimidating astuteness as a critic of poetry is certainly enough to give one pause. In 1928 Graves and Riding collaborated on *A Survey of Modernist Poetry,* an influential work whose exceedingly close textual analyses helped lay the foundations for the New Criticism. Their aim was to mediate between the new poetry and the "plain reader," though it is soon evident that it is the plain reader who had better watch his step. They begin by subjecting a poem by E. E. Cummings, "Sunset," to an alarming battery of tests, after which they pronounce it sound.[8] I am unable to agree with this conclusion: to me, the poem is a tired example of 1920s imagist free verse at its most generic; I should add, though, that I have never been able to enjoy Cummings's poetry. This is no doubt a blind spot which is my problem, but the problem is that everybody is guilty of having blind spots and perpetrating erratic judgments; criticism therefore has to take this into account, yet there is no provision for it in the mathematically precise poetry criticism of Graves and Riding. They are much funnier when they are trashing or thrashing poetry that deserves it, as they do in their next book, *A Pamphlet against Anthologies*.

To give an idea of how intimidating is the critical intelligence that breathes down one's neck when one is reading Riding's poetry, and also of what daily conversations at Deyá must have been like, here are a couple of samples of their vivisection of a popular anthology poem, W. B. Yeats's "Lake Isle of Innisfree":

"I will arise and go now, and go to Innisfree." The name Innisfree is a romantic invention, with the syllable "free" slipped in to help the reader to the conclusion that Innisfree isn't the name of an up-to-date private nursing home or the prodigal's father's house; but an island refuge, somewhere remote and solitary, in Ireland of the legends. "And a small cabin build there, of clay and wattles made." The smallness of the cabin suggests the complete enervation of the poet who could not even trouble to build himself a roomy retreat, and his complete improvidence against the damp of an Irish winter . . . The most miserable touch is the proposal to *build* a cabin which he magically finds already *made* before he reaches the end of the line: suggesting the wish-fulfillment mechanism of the ordinary fatigue-dream.

A bit farther on they dissect the line, "While I stand on the roadway, or on the pavements grey":

Is there an antithesis between the roadway and the pavement? If
so, it is not clearly made. And how does "while I stand" square
with "I will arise"? Perhaps he stood on the roadway but sat on
the pavement. Why the "pavement gray"? Is that an inversion
for the sake of the rhyme, or does gray refer predicatively to the
poet? Why all the "ay" sounds? Are they intended to create a
melancholy urban sound in contrast with the Tennysonian
vowel variation of the preceding line; or is it just carelessness,
and is the internal rhyme of "way" and "gray" unintentional?[9]

Though it should now be obvious why anyone would
think twice before crossing critical pens with Riding, I have
to say that her own poetry is no more exempt from negative
criticism than anybody else's. Franz Kafka in his diaries has a
fragment of a short story about a certain man named Gustav
Blenkelt; he says of him, "As there are everywhere, there
were people who admired him, people who honored him,
people who put up with him, and, finally, those who wanted
to have nothing to do with him."[10] This pretty much sums up
my feelings about Laura Riding's poetry. I find much of it
incomprehensible, some of it extraordinarily beautiful, and
some of it terrible. My inability to understand it does not
affect my assessments of its beauty or ugliness. I should point
out that Wexler's study of Riding includes many painstaking
exegeses of the poems, but I find most of these as difficult to
follow as the poems themselves. The study was written with
Riding's cooperation, so it is possible that many of the expli-
cations came straight from the horse's mouth, so to speak.
However, after reading an early draft of her manuscript, Rid-
ing broke off relations with Wexler, who tells us: "I felt she

was disappointed to find a gap between her sense of her life and the image I presented. In her final letter, she asked why interpretations and explanations were necessary at all. Were her words not good enough in themselves? They are indeed; there is no substitute for reading her work. But criticism never attempts to supplant its subject."[11] One feels sympathy for both parties. It is every poet's dream for his or her own words to supplant possible criticism, poetry being in itself a kind of criticism, and never more so than in the case of Laura Riding. Yet poetry is also somehow incomplete without the external completion of it by a reader/critic, hence the dilemma of the critic who identifies so deeply with the poet as to feel he has absorbed the latter's task.

Since 1929 was a watershed year in both Riding's life and her work, it might be helpful to look now at the work of her so clearly defined early period. The youthful poems published in *The Fugitive,* not all of which were collected later, are from the beginning stamped by the rigor that was to be a constant, which appealed so strongly to Tate and his colleagues and which must have struck an extraordinarily new note at the time. There is very little in the way of music, rhetoric, or picture-making; the lines are as clipped and concentrated as those of Imagist poetry, but they seldom offer us images. A startling exception is the poem "Saturday Night," which was not reprinted until Laura Riding included it in the appendix of the 1980 reprint edition of her 1938 *Collected Poems;* in the preface to that reprint, she speaks of it as having "the stamp upon it of American location," and says that she wrote it at the age of twenty-two or twenty-three and

that it "has for background scenes that had remained vivid
after about seventeen years in my memory-pictures of expe-
riences of my childhood—when I would make free to slip
away on Saturday nights from my parents' place of business
in a Pennsylvania town for peeks at what was going on in the
streets."[12] This peep into her past offered by Riding is as
unique as the poem is in her *oeuvre*. It has a kind of Spoon
River or Winesburg flavor which would never reappear; it is
also a kind of hail and farewell to contemporary poetry of
that time, and worth quoting from as an example of what
her work did not become:

> The farmers' wives and all the wives in town,
> The husbands, the young men who watch the feet
> Of women as if they were afraid that they
> Might blush through looking at the rest of them,
> The old men spitting kindly at the gutters,
> And all the sad Salvation Army folk
> (There must be more than faith to keep the voice
> Of that Salvation Army lass so high
> Above the crowds that pass indifferently),
> And yet besides, bewildered dogs and children—
> I wonder if they like to think they've come
> To heaven at last, that they parade vaguely
> Among themselves like ghosts, knowing that ghosts
> Are silent and unseen, and they themselves
> Bedimmed in the store shadows on Saturday nights.[13]

There are a few traces here of what her writing would
become—in the grotesque wit (as in "The old men spitting

kindly at the gutters"); in her comment on the Salvation
Army girl's high-pitched voice; and in the spectral city with
its crowds of ghosts—but the almost conventional narrative
tone used to depict a genre scene would henceforth be dis-
pensed with, as Riding sought to reduce poetry to the bare
bones of thought. Yet her poems are far from cerebral.
Wexler says that "thought is often considered abstract, but
Laura Riding considered thought the most intense aspect of
life . . . She made her poetry a record of her mind becoming
aware of itself. Convinced she was accomplishing something
new, she avoided using common poetic devices such as anal-
ogy, allusion, or sensory imagery. Her response to her aware-
ness of her thoughts was neither vague nor general, and there
is nothing abstract about her poems . . . Even poems about
love and lust express the speaker's mental response to her
feelings."[14]

Here, for instance, is Riding on sex, from a short prose
piece entitled "Sex, Too" from her book *Experts Are Puzzled:*
"Sex, too, has a meaning, or rather sex is embarrassment of
meaning: it is an awkward way of going about things. It is a
roundabout way of arriving at a point that could not be
found if it were aimed at directly—could not yet be found.
For sex is a slowness; it is a not being too soon; it is a go-
ing to be; it is instead of sleeping; it is a wide-awake sleeping,
a sleepy readiness for waking."[15] Despite the abstract lan-
guage with its avoidance of concrete nouns or adjectives,
what Riding gives us here is an almost physical sensation
of the act of sex, rendered through the medium of thought
transmuted into poetry; even the seesawing rhythms of
the clauses contribute to the accuracy of the impression

conveyed, which is still anything but sensuous. Extreme accuracy is the note of her work, here as always, and if we find her work difficult, as we frequently shall, we are often willing to give her the benefit of the doubt and conclude, as she tells us elsewhere, that what looks like difficulty in her poetry is really accuracy.

This is perhaps as good a place as any to mention a conversation I had once with Seamus Heaney, a poet who like me feels he was not put on earth to lecture on poetry, but who, in his case, does so admirably well. I mentioned the relative unfamiliarity of the poets I had chosen to discuss in these lectures, and how I would have liked to give listeners more of a feel for their work by reading from it. He said, "Yes, but you feel that would be cheating because you're supposed to be talking *about* poems and analyzing them. But go ahead and read them the poetry—they like that." With his authorization, then, I'm going to present some examples of Laura Riding's poetry: the beautiful and the bad, with my intended emphasis on the first category.

The bad news first. Here are two sonnets from a series of five called "Sonnets in Memory of Samuel."

I

His face dripped not like rain on his cravat
But junketed, for that he took his job
So apoplectically not spittle but fat
Flowed foaming from the mandibles of the slob.
He fed of sixth sense to a fine pot-belly
Of psychological stew and he was sick
Of hasty pudding love for all and nobody,

Was sinister with silk and pudgy with brick;
Never knew whether it was love or the jaundice
That drained his gills and flushed his goiter yellow;
Never was devised for simple human service,
Was a lout at play and such a clumsy fellow.
And yet his verses were neither grease nor bad
As some that better loins and liver had.

IV

His critics, in their thin and early twenties,
Pronounced him, fat and forty, a wonder-child,
Blind to the age of his simplicities,
Not seeing, if he was fat, so was Oscar Wilde.
So he wed his laundress, not thinking of Rousseau.
But because she recognized his *furor poeticus*
Boiling among her suds, while his critics could go
No further than their literary Leviticus.
Heavens, he was fat, wept much, fretted, fumed, and
    scribbled,
Did not compose in a rural tedium in the city,
Abandoned Freud on his wedding day, was ribald,
Like an honest man, with his wife but never in poetry.
Is it any wonder Samuel's *p*'s and *q*'s
Did not appear in any of the reviews?[16]

We do not know who this Samuel is, though he is the subject
of two poems preceding this sonnet sequence, all in Riding's
first book, *The Close Chaplet*. Unlike the prophet Samuel, he
was "never devised for simple human service." He has a Jew-
ish name, and many of the disgusting details in the first

sonnet suggest an anti-Semitic caricature of a Jew. Is anti-Semitism part of the content of the poem? Did she despise her father's race as well as his politics? This would have been useful to know so as to construe the poem, which is otherwise pretty unconstruable and offers neither the traditional goodies of poetry which Riding scorns nor the intellectual rigor she espouses—at least as far as I can tell. "And yet his verses were neither grease nor bad / as some that better loins and liver had." Is she making an antithesis between poetry that is grease and poetry that is as bad as that of poets with better digestive tracts, and if so, why?

In the fourth sonnet, why do Samuel's thin critics pronounce him, fat and forty, a wonder child? In what way are they blind to the age of his simplicities, whatever that is; not seeing, if he was fat, so was Oscar Wilde? Does that mean that Wilde was of the age of simplicities? One doesn't associate Wilde with simplicities; but if Samuel resembled him in being simple as well as fat, why didn't the critics see this? What was it in this state of affairs that caused him to wed his laundress, not thinking of Rousseau, but because his laundress recognized his *furor poeticus* boiling among her suds? What was it doing there? Was it a humdrum but agitated thing like soapsuds? In that case, why was he never ribald in poetry? How did the suds prevent that? Why did he marry her because his critics could go no further than their literary Leviticus, and who was that? Wilde or Rousseau? Both might be characterized as "laying down the law," but as stringently as Leviticus?

He, Samuel, was fat, wept much, fretted, fumed, and scribbled, but did not compose in a rural tedium in the city. Isn't this true of most poets who live in cities? If he abandoned

Freud on his wedding day, how come he was ribald with his wife, and what does that have to do with never being ribald in poetry? And why did his p's and q's, meaning scruples, not appear in any of the reviews? Reviews don't publish scruples. Or if she intends by that phrase scrupulous poetry, why didn't it appear in reviews since the critics had already pronounced him a wonder child? If I feel it is worthwhile applying a few of Riding's own strictures to this poetry, it's because I feel that even if I understood it, it would be a lame thing, unsalvageable through critical exegesis and worthless even if it were. (In fairness, it should be pointed out that Riding never reprinted these sonnets in later collections and so perhaps did not esteem them very highly herself.)

Here, on the other hand, is another example from the same early volume, one which is almost lush, or to use a word that Riding uses to disparage lyrical poetry, flesh-some. The opening lines almost suggest some minor Elizabethan lyricist, a Nash or a Dowland:

No More Are Lovely Palaces

No more are lovely palaces
And Taj-Mahal is old.
The listening tenements,
The longing entertainments
Waited wide and many ages
For the spirits of the promises
That more than men would come,
Would come the visitants evoked
By lovely palaces
And such emblazoned places
Men would never light for men.

No more is slaughtered stone
Or listed stubborn marble
To make an open hostel.
The spirits will not dwell,
Are present never in the sepulchres,
Scarcely whisper past the minarets
Or set a foot upon the doorsteps.

A little surer now we know
They do not come the way we go.
And better build we and more soberly
Houses fitter far to leave
Than to receive
As guests the hovering hosts
Of the hospitable ghosts

That swing death's doors
And suck us into topless palaces
Terrific on the blowing bluish spaces
Where we gasp out our gratitude
And say breathless:
Heaven's hand is not gentle,
The lovely palaces were too lovely,
The most victorious lavish is the most terrible.[17]

Here the idea seems to be that we no longer build grandly, for the spirits avoid our constructed grandeur, which we do not intend for mere men. Spirits avoid the sepulchers and minarets we thought would content them. So now we build more soberly; our houses are better fit to leave than to receive hospitable ghosts, who nevertheless suck us up through death's door into a high place where we can only gasp out our gratitude and acknowledge that heaven's hand is not gentle; the lovely palaces erred in being just that, too lovely; the "most victorious lavish" to which we have been transplanted—heaven, apparently—is most terrible since its lavish is victorious: it has subsumed us into a grandeur we don't want and in which we cannot live. At least, that may be her meaning; to me, it doesn't matter because the overwhelmingly spare and beautiful language has already satisfied me.

Since the loveliest palaces were too lovely, it is only natural that the poems for which we most value Riding are far from the "victorious lavish" mode of the previous poem. More typical and ultimately more satisfying are such seemingly unlovely poems as "Unread Pages" and "The Unthronged Oracle," whose titles may reflect her view of herself. Discussing the latter poem, Barbara Adams points out that as an oracle, Riding was far from unthronged, at least in Deyá, where she was "the center of a flurry of disciples who came from England and America to sit at the feet of Graves, but who ended up in impromptu poetry workshops directed by Riding at their Majorcan home."[18] In Adams's reading of "The Unthronged Oracle," Riding "looks to herself as the oracle within, giving herself answers that do not satisfy. . . . She remains cut off from her own oracular self by also being part of material reality: 'newspapers, mirrors, birds and births and clocks / Divide you from her by a trembling film . . .'" One could dwell further on this odd and brilliant choice of objects which here exemplify "material reality": birds, for instance, who make frequent ambiguous appearances throughout Riding's poetry, starting with the very first line in

"A Bird Speaks," the first poem in her posthumous collection of early poetry, *First Awakenings:* "You think I am a pretty little bird, don't you . . ." Mirrors are omnipresent too, as in another early poem, "For One Who Will Keep a Mirror." Riding herself "kept" mirrors; for all her austerity she was apparently fastidious with regard to clothes and jewelry. Judging from photographs, she had devised a "look"—both fanciful and demure—that must have been recognizably hers. So she may indeed have felt that mirrors like those in the line quoted by Adams divided her from "her own oracular self."

   Here is "Unread Pages," a poem in the same crabbed, almost exasperated tone as "The Unthronged Oracle," but which also reveals its riches gradually.

   An end is a happy end only:
   What only was moves into what is,
   Unbodied grows, but lasting.
   And the matter is now alive,
   Even by this beneficence of Yes
   To No and No like angels made of nothing.

   Science, the white heart of strangers,
   Bleeds with an immaculate grief—
   Impatient brotherhood,
   Tired apostates of curiosity,
   Creed of apostatizing.
   Truth need be but dead afterworld
   To those who've had enough,

The readers and the lookers-on—
As stars keep off, or to short minds
Night seems a less real time than day,
Not to be measured with or counted to
That quick self-evident sum of sun.

Have sleep and midnight warmth,
Where your scant eyes see failure,
Numbering the wakefullest page
The dark and frosty last.

An end is a happy end only.
And first the book's end comes,
The printed public leaves off reading.

Then open the small secret doors,
When none's there to read awrong.
Out runs happiness in a crowd,
The saving words and hours
That come too tragic-late for souls
Gifted with their own mercy:
Who spare themselves the joys
that would have darkened them
From the predaceous years.

Too orthodox maturity
For such heresy of child-remaining—
On these the dusty blight of books descends,
Weird, pundit babyhoods
Whose blinking vision stammers out the past
Like a big-lettered foetus-future.[19]

Riding may have felt herself unthronged and unread, but this was at least partially her intention. She ends her introduction to *First Awakenings* thus: "Not even good-willed purpose to see in the whole [*sic*] could be safe from going astray in the ramifications of exegetically thorough attention either to my Collected Poems as a body of poetic particularities, the mastering of them expected to be generally illuminating critically and personally, or to the additionally available archival poetic material, or to the composite bulk of both units of quantity arbitrarily construed as constituting my poetic work as a whole."[20] Thus warned, we may cautiously approach "Unread Pages" both for the superb poem it is and for what it may have to tell us about its author. She begins by announcing that "an end is a happy end only," as "what only was moves into what is." Stories and poems inhabit the fictive land of "was"; it is at this point that "the printed public" (readers still partly mired in text) "leaves off reading." Truth *need be* but dead afterworld as far as these "dead apostates of curiosity" are concerned, these subscribers to lending libraries enamored of literary baubles, "short minds" who have "had enough" and are indifferent to truth though not unwilling to ingest it should it turn up in the course of their reading. "As stars keep off" (in her beautiful formulation) and these "common readers" sink into sleep and midnight warmth, they number the wakefullest page as the "dark and frosty" last.

Despite this deceptive *finis* that brings the reader peace, albeit a not entirely wholesome one ("peace in a time of peace," in Wallace Stevens's phrase), the reading or some related kind of activity keeps on happening when "none's there to read awrong." (That would probably refer to most of her readership.) "Happiness in a crowd" somehow escapes through the "small secret doors" she will have opened, though it's too "tragic-late" for the readers. A crowd of what, or whom? And what are these doors? In any case, another situation, beyond reading perhaps, unavailable to those who would have ended up "darkened" by joys they have spared themselves. "From the predaceous years" is a further ambiguity. Have the self-pitying souls unknowingly escaped the smudging depredations of time by careless reading, or are they themselves somehow sparing the joys from all-devouring time? In either case, these miniature pundits would have ended up with a too orthodox, hence false, kind of maturity, suited to their infantile, "big-lettered" reading, as the breathtakingly ugly last time (a more efficacious ugliness than that of the Samuel sonnets) makes clear. The pages that come after the numbered, wakefullest one remain unread, but that is our loss, not theirs: they live on in starlit integrity, "happiness in a crowd." They do not communicate, leaving that falsifying task to their numbered predecessors. The poem as a whole anticipates a statement about poetry that Riding would make years later in *The Telling*: "Poetry is a sleep-maker which sits up late in us listening for the footfall of the future on today's doorstep."[21]

I mentioned earlier that Laura Riding once took me to task in a letter for daring to say publicly that I felt I had been influenced by her. I have since found that I am in good company. Even Robert Graves was taken to task for this. Wexler tells us that Riding denied that she influenced anyone except her husband, that anyone had in fact followed her principles of conduct.[22] Especially angered at Graves's apparently gallant tributes to her, Riding accused him of lifting ideas from her work yet failing to assimilate their import. She was most contemptuous of W. H. Auden, who always acknowledged her influence and whose work of the 1930s would have been quite different without the example of Riding's pared-down, quicksilver metaphysics: think of "Law, say the gardeners, is the sun"; or the poems beginning, "This lunar beauty / has no history / is complete and early"; and "Jumbled in the common box of their dark stupidity / Orchid swan and Caesar lie."[23] John Wheelwright, though he wrote a dismissive review of Riding, must also have been influenced by her. As for me, here is an early poem of mine; I cite it not because it's a favorite, but because it seems marked by Riding's concision more than others more satisfying to me, poems in which her influence is more diffuse.

The Thinnest Shadow

He is sherrier
And sherriest.
A tall thermometer
Reflects him best.
Children in the street
Watch him go by.
"Is that the thinnest shadow?"
They to one another cry.

A face looks from the mirror
As if to say,

"Be supple, young man,
Since you can't be gay."

All his friends have gone
From the street corner cold.
His heart is full of lies
And his eyes are full of mold.[24]

One must misread Riding in order to be enriched by her. One must ignore her promises of future enlightenment, the pie in the sky which will turn out to be better than poetry ever could be. T. S. Matthews, a member of the Graves–Riding set in both Deyá and New Hope, who introduced Jackson to Riding, presents a less than flattering picture of her in his book of literary reminiscences, *Jacks and Better.* After Jackson's death, he says, though it was obvious that their magnum opus on linguistics would never see the light of day, Riding "would admit no such thing, and instead threw out hints that [it] was in large part completed and might some day soon appear." "In such promissory utterances," he says, "particularly in a small book called *The Telling,* Laura, like a sideshow barker, held out the promise of great things, marvelous things, to be seen and experienced inside the tent; and like all such performances, hers ended before a single customer had entered. Her spiel carried a tone that was peremptory, overblown and meaningless, at the same time awesome and nonsensical. It was like hearing the veritable voice of God (or its plausible facsimile) in a dream caused by indigestion."[25]

But perhaps the last word should be left to Julian Symons, who ran afoul of Riding merely through asking her for a poem for an anthology: "It is hard to avoid a note of comedy in writing about her—and indeed why should one avoid it? Yet that is not the note to end on in considering her achievement. It was not possible to talk to her without appreciating the power of her intellect, the self-destructive simplicity of her mind. Her Jewish tailor father hoped that she would become an American Rosa Luxembourg. She became instead (so long as silence permits a valediction) a sort of saint of poetry and like all saints, tiresome; but what she did, by her work and her example, to purify poetic language, could have been done in no other way, and perhaps by no other kind of person. There are many who owe her a debt."[26]

VI

⌃ David Schubert

"This Is the Book That No One Knows"

In 1983, the *Quarterly Review of Literature* celebrated its fortieth anniversary by publishing a book of writings by and about David Schubert, a little-known poet whom both the editors, Theodore and Renée Weiss, had known during the 1930s. I contributed a short essay to the collection, in which I made the remark: "To sit down for a little while and reread some of Schubert's rare and poignant verse is like opening a window in a room that had become stuffy without one's realizing it."[1]

As I was writing the present chapter, almost by chance I came across a letter from William Carlos Williams to Theodore Weiss which was not included in the Schubert memorial volume. Williams wrote, "Many thanks for the Schubert poems, they are first rate—more than that, far more. They are among the few poems I read that belong in the new anthology—where neither Eliot nor, I am afraid, Pound belong. I wish I could get up that anthology where the rails are polished silver they are so clear in the sunlight I should provide. There is, you know, a physically new poetry which almost no one as yet has sensed. Schubert is a nova in that sky. I hope I am not using hyperbole to excess. You know how it is when someone opens a window on a stuffy room."[2]

Needless to say, I was quite delighted and surprised to find that Dr. Williams and I had hit on the same phrase to describe the effect Schubert's poetry had for us, or rather that I had fortuitously used the same expression some forty years after Williams. And not just because it seemed to justify my having chosen an important occasion such as a lecture in the Norton series to talk about a poet whom almost nobody has ever heard of. It also seemed a kind of justification for the theme of these lectures, which I began by calling "The Other Tradition," and, when that began to sound a little pompous, backed down and decided to name it "Another Tradition," then finally and more accurately, "Other Traditions." It shores up my feeling that the poets (and of course this could apply to people in any line of endeavor) who become known and are remembered and put in anthologies are there as much from happenstance as intrinsic merit. Perhaps it is a little truer of poets than of others because poetry is a somewhat neglected art to begin with; it has trouble making its way in the best of circumstances, and there are not too many judges monitoring the situation to make sure each one gets what he or she deserves. Poems get lost more easily than paintings do; even their authors tend to forget them in drawers or sometimes destroy them in a fit of rage, as Schubert in fact did with a large body of his work, including a novel whose first sentence alone survives: "Outside it was Tuesday."[3]

I myself value Schubert more than Pound or Eliot, and it's a relief to have an authority of the stature of Williams to

back me up. For we believe in what survives; that which falls
by the wayside, for whatever reason, cannot interest us.
Schubert didn't help matters by going insane and alienating
the few people who knew and believed in his poetry; he was
constantly dogged by bad luck. But things could so easily
have been different. He wrote during the Great Depression,
when every poet, indeed everybody, was having a hard time.
Had he managed to hang on to life a little longer (he died
from tuberculosis in 1946 at the age of thirty-three) he
surely, with the help of Dr. Williams and others who admired
him, including Robert Frost, James Laughlin, and Morton
Dauwen Zabel, would have found his audience, perhaps
would even have been recognized as the American Arthur
Rimbaud or Osip Mandelstam, as I think he deserves to be.
But how does it happen that I am here telling you this? If it
hadn't been for the coincidence that, thirty-five years ago,
W. H. Auden heard from a friend that both Frank O'Hara
and I had submitted to the Yale Younger Poets competition
and had our manuscripts returned by Yale University Press,
then asked to see them and chose mine for publication
(somewhat reluctantly, I have reason to believe; he was
apparently not really enthusiastic about either entry but
found them slightly preferable to those that had been for-
warded to him), I might not have had a volume of poetry
published and eventually been deemed a worthy recipient for
the honor of giving the Norton Lectures. No one has written
about the precariousness of our careers better than Auden,
and I'd like to quote a passage from Caliban's speech in *The
Sea and the Mirror,* after which I will have done with the

vanity of human wishes and proceed to Schubert's poetry. "So, too," Auden writes,

with Time, who, in our auditorium, is not her dear old buffer so anxious to please everybody, but a prim magistrate whose court never adjourns, and from whose decisions, as he laconically sentences one to loss of hair and talent, another to seven days' chastity, and a third to boredom for life, there is no appeal. We should not be sitting here now, washed, warm, well-fed, in seats we have paid for, unless there were others who are not here; our liveliness and good humour, such as they are, are those of survivors, conscious that there are others who have not been so fortunate, others who did not succeed in navigating the narrow passage or to whom the natives were not friendly, others whose streets were chosen by the explosion or through whose country the famine turned aside from ours to go, others who failed to repel the invasion of bacteria or to crush the insurrection of their bowels, others who lost their suit against their parents or were ruined by wishes they could not adjust or murdered by resentments they could not control; aware of some who were better and bigger but from whom, only the other day, Fortune withdrew her hand in sudden disgust, now nervously playing chess with drunken sea-captains in sordid cafés on the equator or the Arctic Circle, or lying, only a few blocks away, strapped and screaming on iron beds or dropping to naked pieces in damp graves. And shouldn't you too, dear master, reflect—forgive us for mentioning it—that we might very well not have been attending a production of yours this evening, had not some other and maybe—who can tell?—brighter talent married a barmaid or turned religious and shy or gone down in a liner with all his manuscripts, the loss recorded only in the corner of some country newspaper below A Poultry Lover's Jottings?[4]

Not much is known about Schubert's early life; his wife said that he always refused to talk about it. He was born in Brooklyn in 1913 but grew up in Detroit. His parents were very poor. When he was about twelve, his father abandoned the family, and his mother committed suicide soon after; apparently Schubert discovered her body when he came home from school. He, his sister, and his brother were then raised by various relatives. The biographical note on him in the New Directions volume *Five Young American Poets* for 1941 states that he was homeless from the age of fifteen, supporting himself by selling newspapers and working as a busboy, soda jerk, farm hand, and various other jobs. One thinks of the lines from his poem "No Title," which Frank O'Hara quoted in his poem "For David Schubert": "I stood there on Forty-Second Street and Eighth Avenue. I stood there with two nickels."[5] Schubert attended Boys High School in Brooklyn, where he was an excellent student; at sixteen, he received a full scholarship to Amherst College. His strange personality both impressed and exasperated his teachers there, who included Robert Frost and the poet John Theobald. (According to Judith Schubert, his widow, Frost supported Schubert for a while with a stipend of three dollars a week.)[6] One of Schubert's teachers, Theodore Baird, remembers that "already as a freshman he was experimenting with language, playing with words, turning them round, letting them slide off into other meanings. . . . David Schubert had only one language, the one he was exploring with such inward delight, and he used it for all occasions, whether writing a poem or a history paper or a botany quiz."[7]

Dropped from Amherst, reinstated thanks to special pleading from his teachers, and ultimately dropped again, Schubert ignored his studies and worked almost constantly on his poetry.

Meanwhile, he had met the woman he would eventually marry, on a country road in the Berkshires. Judith Schubert, née Ehre, recalls their meeting: "Molly and I were sitting on a Monterey, Massachusetts, lawn, on a very hot August day in 1932, munching the berries we had gathered, while we tried to hitch a ride back to our inn. Neither of us noticed the figure that emerged from the house behind the trees until we heard the crackling of leaves made by the moccasined feet of the young man who approached us; he sat down on a rock a little distance away. About five feet eight, and very slender, his tan corduroy jacket, brown slacks and dark blue shirt open at the throat were far from outlandish. Probably it was his enigmatic smile, and the way he looked through us with his extraordinarily large dark blue eyes, that suggested some non-being from a Tennyson idyll."[8] David wrote about their fateful interview in a (for him) remarkably direct poem called "Monterey."

> The hills were lush
> With rain and youth. I did
> What chores were my portion
> In the shack I shared with two friends.
> It was to be for us
> A landmark in our lives, a moment
> When we were tired out, when
> We didn't have anything else to

Do. What a home and parents should
Be.
    She came with a friend,
Calling, on the road. She was
Dissatisfied with her lodging.
One of us met them on the
Road, invited them in for lunch.

      I loved her not
For herself, but for myself. She
Was, of girls imagined, one.

      I am a rugged individualist;
I did not tarry or pretend.[9]

After an on-again, off-again courtship, they were married in
1933.

During the 1930s, they lived in a picturesque garret in
Brooklyn Heights overlooking New York Harbor. David
eventually got a degree from City College and held various
jobs, but the couple were mainly supported by Judith's salary
as a schoolteacher. They became friends with the poets
Theodore Weiss, Ben Belitt, Horace Gregory, and Marya
Zaturenska, as well as the painter Mark Rothko. In the mid-
1930s, David began to publish his poetry in such magazines
as *The Nation, Partisan Review,* and the *Virginia Quarterly
Review*; in 1936, he was awarded *Poetry* magazine's Jean-
nette Sewell Davis Prize for a young poet. But mental illness
had set in, and with it the deterioration of the Schuberts'
marriage. Sometimes David would disappear, penniless, for
days or weeks. Early in 1943, after a particularly violent

scene, Judith felt she was no longer safe living with him; she left, and it was at that point that David destroyed all his papers (which Judith would later spend years trying to piece back together), as well as a painting Rothko had given them. After several weeks, he turned up in a mental hospital in Washington, D.C., where he had gone, he said, "to see Archibald MacLeish and get into the navy."[10] Judith managed to get him transferred to Bloomingdale Hospital in White Plains, where he was diagnosed as a paranoid schizophrenic. Eventually he was transferred to a hospital in Central Islip, Long Island, where he died of tuberculosis on April 1, 1946. Judith remarried after his death. In 1961, after numerous rejections from publishers, she managed to publish his collection *Initial A* with Macmillan.[11] The poems in that volume were reprinted with many previously unpublished ones, as well as letters, critical essays, and biographical reminiscences, in the 1983 *Quarterly Review of Literature* collection, which is called *David Schubert: Works and Days*.

Wallace Stevens, whom Schubert admired, wrote that "the poem must resist the intelligence / almost successfully." Much of Schubert's poetry stretches that "almost" almost to the snapping point, and in doing so manages to render itself immune to critical analysis or even paraphrase. How then does one discuss Schubert, or more precisely, how does one talk about him to an audience of whom few will likely have read his work? Not, I think, in the way of Irvin Ehrenpreis, who contributed the longest essay to *Works and Days*. Auden's Caliban speaks of "the academic fields to be guarded with umbrella and learned periodical against the trespass of any unqualified stranger, not a whit less jealously than the game preserve is protected from the poacher by the unamiable shotgun,"[12] and it is from this secure vantage point that Ehrenpreis proceeds to construe these ultimately unconstruable poems, identifying their mysterious contents, supplying autobiographical contexts which are arguable to say the least, locating Schubert's bare pedestal in the sculpture garden of twentieth-century poetry, and sending him on his way with the recommendation: "It is time we saluted the poet as a rightful heir of Stevens, Eliot, and Crane."[13] Rachel Hadas, herself a fine poet, has written what is to date the most intelligent essay on Schubert, a review of *Works and Days* in *Parnassus,* and she rightly takes this conclusion to task: "Despite undisputed echoes of these poets in Schubert's work, the truest and most helpful way to praise him is not to jimmy his name into a Great Tradition. Instead we should try to grasp and convey his most immediate and most enduring legacy: the strange originality of his poetry."[14]

Let's try to do that then, with and without Ehrenpreis's academic measuring tools and not losing sight of Hadas's important caveats. Ehrenpreis has chosen several poems of Schubert that represent major stages in his career, the first being "Kind Valentine," which launched his career with the prize from *Poetry* and is also one of the most beautiful poems he ever wrote.

> She hugs a white rose to her heart—
> The petals flare—in her breath blown;
> She'll catch the fruit on her death day—
> The flower rooted in the bone.

The face at evening comes for love;
Reeds in the river meet below.
She sleeps small child, her face a tear;
The dream comes in with stars to go
Into the window, feigning snow.
This is the book that no one knows.
The paper wall holds mythic oaks,
Behind the oaks a castle grows.
Over the door, and over her
(She dies! she wakes!) the steeds gallop.
The child stirs, hits the dumb air, weeps,
Afraid of night's long loving-cup.

Into yourself, live, Joanne!
And count the buttons—how they run
To doctor, red chief, lady's man!
Most softly pass, on the stairs down,
The stranger in your evening gown.
Hearing white, inside your grief,
An insane laughter up the roof.
O little wind, come in with dawn—
It is your shadow on the lawn.

Break the pot! and let carnations—
Smell them! they're the very first.
Break the sky and let come magic
Rain! Let earth come pseudo-tragic
Roses—blossom, unrehearsed.
Head, break! is broken. Dream, so small,
Come in to her. O little child,
Dance on squills where the winds run wild.

The candles rise in the warm night
Back and forth, the tide is bright.
Slowly, slowly, the waves retreat
Under her wish and under feet.
And over tight breath, tighter eyes,
The mirror ebbs, it ebbs and flows.
And the intern, the driver, speed
To gangrene! But—who knows—suppose
He was beside her! Please, star-bright,
First I see, while in the night
A soft-voiced, like a tear, guitar—
It calls a palm coast from afar.
And oh, so far the stars were there
For him to hang upon her hair
Like the white rose he gave, white hot,
While the low sobbing band—it wept
Violets and forget-me-nots.[15]

Hadas says that Ehrenpreis "tells us more than we need to know, quite possibly more than is there ('Joanne as a sad child, then as a girl dangerously in love, next as a psychotic mourning the loss of her mysterious lover, and so as a suicide and last as a corpse.')" She goes on, "None of all this touches upon what makes this startling poem unique: its rhythmic verve, bouncing pace, and magical blend of tones, declamatory and elegiac, hysterical and tender, all at once. The diction teeters on the brink of camp, yet manages to be moving anyway." Elsewhere she mentions that "many of Schubert's poems seem to consist of slivers gracefully or haphazardly fitted together. Such fragments rarely combine to form a larger structure or texture: images, rhythms, narrative stance, and syntax keep shifting, but most strikingly slippery is tone."[16]

We know from Schubert's widow that he was a chain smoker and was always writing down fragments of poetry in the matchbooks he carried with him, which he would later incorporate into his poems. The typical Schubert poem has the appearance of something smashed, not too painstakingly put back together again, and finally contemplated with both remorse and amusement. In this, it resembles many of the elements of his life: his marriage, his failed attempts at education and employment, his inability to connect with people who were trying to help him. (Judith Schubert reported that Frost would willingly have provided him with both financial and critical help in his later, desperate years but that Schubert was too proud to ask for it.) These are like pieces of life, quick and articulate no matter how grotesquely reassembled. "Kind Valentine" seems to me not a poem about the stages of life awaiting a young girl, but an address to a girl who is slipping in and out of dreams by a poet similarly afflicted. Much of its effect comes from slight dislocations of grammar, so that one's expectations are constantly in a tense state. For example: "This is the book that no one knows. / The paper wall holds mythic oaks, / Behind the oaks a castle grows." (Is this an allusion perhaps to the growing castle in August Strindberg's *Dream Play*, whose subject is the failure of communication between men and gods?) And then: "Over the door, and over her / (She dies! She wakes!) the steeds gallop." We might expect the steeds to gallop through the door and over her, but dreams, nightmares no doubt in this case, have their own rules of dimension and perspective and their own inscrutable reasons for having them. In any case, the steeds' disorderly and hence disturbing arrival in the room foreshadows the quite possibly sinister nature of the contents of "night's long loving-cup." The poet then commands Joanne to live "into yourself." In a letter to Ben Belitt, Schubert wrote: "Frost once said to me that—a poet—his arms can go out—like this—or in to himself; in either case he will cover a good deal of the world";[17] perhaps Schubert feels at this point that Joanne will cover the world most effectively by living "into" herself. The rest of the stanza, in which Joanne is told to count buttons to the tune of a childish rhyme and then pass down the stairs and onto the lawn, hearing "an insane laughter up the roof"—here again the phrase is slightly askew, as though the laughter were coming from someone not on the roof but perhaps wedged under it and who was insane enough to set the roof slightly ajar so as to be audible to someone on the ground below—the rest seems to me, *pace* Ehrenpreis, not a further stage in Joanne's maturing into a girl dangerously in love but merely an extension of the dream, which is plotless like all dreams. Although Joanne in counting buttons is to think successively of "doctor, red chief, lady's man," all possible suitors, there is a real confusion in the next lines—"Most softly pass, on the stairs down, / The stranger in your evening gown"—as to who is wearing the evening gown: Joanne herself as a child or later on as a young woman; another woman who might be her rival for the suitors' attentions; one of the suitors, even; or—

such is the unaccountability of dreams—an amalgam of all three.

The first line of the next stanza is an uncompleted thought, a figure of rhetoric called aposiopesis, of which the classic example is Neptune's "Quos ego" warning to the winds in the *Aeneid*. "Break the pot! and let carnations— / Smell them! they're the very first." Why break the pot in order to smell the carnations? Let them do what? And why are they the very first? We don't think of them as a seasonal flower, like the violets and forget-me-nots in the last stanza, but rather as something from the florist's, a first corsage for the girl from a suitor, perhaps, but why the breakage? Something to do with the sacrifice of virginity in order to gain ecstasy? Again, none of this quite adds up, and, in the way of a Schubert poem, it shouldn't: what we are left with is a bouquet of many layered, splintered meanings, to be clasped but never fully understood. As Ehrenpreis says, " 'Kind Valentine' is a splendid accomplishment—compact, obscure and dramatic,"[18] though this is perhaps the only place in his critical writing where obscurity is equated with splendor. Hadas is closer when she says that "what Schubert's best poems capture is the texture of thought itself—ragged, rapid, dancing zigzag from likeness to question and from wish to intention." She says elsewhere: "Schubert is no surrealist; he is poignantly aware that communication cannot be complete and feels the strains between language and meaning as sad or ominous."[19] Surrealism, in abandoning itself to the unconscious, can never accurately reflect experience in which both the conscious and the unconscious play a role: this realization on Schubert's part is indeed one of his unique strengths.

Here is another, apparently later, poem called "Midston House" (though no chronology of Schubert's poems exists, this one seems to have been suggested by job-hunting in the late 1930s):

What is needed is a technique
Of conversation, I think, as I put on the
Electric light. But not the limited
Vocabulary of our experiences, the
Surface irritations which pile up,
Accumulate a city—but the expression,
Metamorphosed, of what they are the
Metaphor of;—and their conversion into light.

On the bus toward Midston House
I survey the people in their actions. Placid
And relaxed are they; this is the humdrum
Claptrap costume of girls and food, men
And work and house. The insurance
Of habit is circular, as
Democracy has interlocking duties,
Circular obediences.

Yet how to transform
The continual failing clouds of
Energy, into light? The vital
Intelligence of the man whom I am
Going to visit—does he know? I
Think of how the sharp severing of
My life's task—severed associations,
Produced in me almost a
Lypothymia of grief and a hiatus of

Days, which grew fangs of anger, my
Lycanthropy—thank god, it's over!

    I am fired from my job by flames, big
As angry consciences: I can do
Nothing: I have not one ability! This man
Whom I am waiting to see in the lobby—
All my life I am waiting for something that
Does not eventuate—will he
Exist?

    The law of life, like an abstract
Rigorous lawyer, passes a terrifying judg-
Ment on poor little me, in a strange foreign
Syllogism. He is cheating me! He will not
Keep the appointment!

      His probity
Rebukes my suspicion. What can I say, that
I love him; that I am un-
Worthy? My doubt makes me feel,
—Even as we discuss another's dishonesty—
Ugly, irate, and damned avid, a cunning
Rascal, like that ugly bird of the White
Nile.

    But the poem is just this
Speaking of what cannot be said
To the person I want to say it.
I am sleepy with subtlety; the room strikes me as
Dark, so cold, so lonely. There is
No one in it. I will put on all the lights.

I wish I could go
On a long, on a long long journey
To a place where life is simple and decent, not
Too demanding.

No! On the vehicle, Tomorrow, I will see
That man, whose handshake was happiness.

On the surface of it, the poet seems to be on his way to meet someone who will offer him a job, at a hotel: I vaguely remember a medium-priced midtown hotel in New York named Midston House, and the solemn nature of being at the midpoint here cannot but suggest the first line of the *Inferno*. Yet again the scenario is broken. First the poet is in a room, turning on a light, though not apparently at Midston House since in the next stanza he is on his way there by bus, where he wonders how to transform the continual failing clouds of energy into light, no such easy business as flicking a switch. Will the man with the vital intelligence know how to transform failure into light? But is that precisely the question? The phrase "continual failing clouds of energy" could mean that the energy is intact even though the clouds that contain it are failing, that these obscuring agents are what it is important to maintain if energy is to become light. The poet then suspects that the man "is cheating me! He will not keep the appointment!" Immediately thereafter, though, his probity rebukes that accusation: the man has kept the appointment; he must now tell the man he loves him and is unworthy. Indeed, he is worse than that—as they discuss the dishonesty of a mysterious third person, Schubert castigates himself as "Ugly, irate, and damned avid, a cunning / Rascal, like that ugly bird of the White / Nile." I don't know what bird he means, but "white" makes me think of Charles Baudelaire's albatross, one of three Baudelaire poems that Schubert translated superbly. It is easy to see why he chose that one: "This traveller, winged, how gauche and weak it is! / It's, lately so handsome, how comical, how homely! / Somebody worries its beak with a short pipe. / Another mimics, limpingly, the sick that flew"—these lines might be Schubert writing about himself. At once, Schubert plunges from the business conversation back into the poem itself: "But the poem is just this / Speaking of what cannot be said / To the person I want to say it," a magnificent definition not only of Schubert's poetry but of poetry itself, and sharpened by the usual slight skewings: there is no colon after "But the poem is just this" though the line breaks there and the ear expects one; similarly, one is tempted to complete the last line by making it: "To the person I want to say it to." That is not what he's saying, however, although it is in a way since he leads us to expect it. The actual sense of the words, though, is that the poem consists of speaking of what cannot be said to the person I want to say it: in other words, the ideal situation for the poet is to have the reader speak the poem. And how nice it would be for everybody if that could be the case. Now, however, the poet is "sleepy with subtlety; the room" is dark, cold, lonely; he "will put on all the lights." "There is no one in it." Is it possible he never left the room at the beginning of the poem, that he imagined the whole encounter? He dreams then of a long journey to a place where life is simple, decent, not too demanding: no

Midston House, apparently, though now he seems to be planning to go there tomorrow: "No! on the vehicle, Tomorrow" ("Tomorrow" is capitalized, leaving the possibility that the vehicle is named Tomorrow, a sort of Streetcar Named Desire, as one critic has suggested), though it may very well be the bus that he may or may not have taken today. Tomorrow, on that vehicle, he "will see that man, whose handshake was happiness." So it seems that he may have met with the man today—his handshake *was* happiness—and, in any case, that he will meet him tomorrow on the bus, saving himself from the painful experience of Midston House, unless the room he has been in all along is indeed in Midston House and the vehicle, the handshake are to be read as rescue from that limbo. It is these multiple points of view and the multiplicity of possible situations that transform the mundane experience of a job interview into one of life's major turning points, where, as Schubert says at the end of his poem "Dissertation on the Detroit Free Press":

> Now as the train rounds a curve, I see
> The engineer who impels our movement.
> Only at the curve, perhaps, do we realize
> The impetus with which our goal is driven.[20]

I'd like to look at another of Schubert's poems, a short one and for me his most beautiful:

> The Visitor
>
> He came from the mountains into this
> Garden. Welcome, sir, all that I have is yours.

He came from the mountains, he spied
The kind shade. He sate with me under the oak tree.

What have you done in the mountains, sir,
Besides hunting the white deer all day?

In the mountains I hunted and I plotted
Your garden's destruction and ruin.

In the mountains I hunted a similitude
To obtain your trusting mood.

Therefore I slay you as
You dream of the friendship I bear.

Said the man from the mountains the mountains
Who came to visit me here.

But I shall, as I look only upward
My star being set in the mountains,

Said the man, the man from the mountains,
See only the fair garden that I murdered here
Said the man the man from the mountains.

Ehrenpreis believes that this is a poem about Schubert's cruel father; since Ehrenpreis knew Judith Schubert well, it's possible that this could be a reading of it, though to do so seems akin to arguing about the identity of the third murderer in *Macbeth*. And why, anyway, should there be but one reading? Once after a poetry reading, I was asked one of those un-questions that people ask poets: "Do you make up your ideas or do they just come to you?" I was so busy wishing I knew the answer that I forgot to ask why both couldn't be the case, and several other things as well. "The Visitor" could as well be a parable of Eden, of Christ accepting the inevitability of martyrdom, or it could be only a story whose meaning is self-contained. The splendor of the landscape and the terribleness of the act remind me of Rimbaud, who was one of Schubert's favorite poets, and also of Lautréamont, whom he may not have known. But the central axis of ambiguity is Schubert's own. The man slays the poet as the latter dreams of the friendship he thought the man bore him. But the murderer suffers perhaps a worse destiny: he will look only upward since his star is set (note the ambiguity of the verb: the star is both fixed and falling) in the mountains. Yet he is fated to see not the star, but instead the fair earthly garden that he murdered down here. Father, friend, or stranger, he is doomed to commit his murder and suffer for it, as his victim is doomed to submit. But as Hadas says, "Even the most cautious psychological speculation is, in a way, beside the point. Schubert's peculiarly incandescent work is in little need of the kind of illumination biography furnishes. His strongest hold on life was through his poems, and it is to the poems that one gratefully turns back."[21] Though there are confessions in the poems—that was one way of holding on to life through them—there is much more besides, which disqualifies him as a "confessional poet." Long before that unfortunate term existed, Schubert made the case against the genre succinctly in a letter to Ben Belitt: "About Crane— what I meant when I said that about 'being cheated' was this: I hate to feel that a poetry is so inextricably tied up with the tragedy of the poet that it cannot lead its own life."[22]

I'd like to end by presenting three poems of Schubert's which give a little more of his range, notably his humor, as in the first one which is called "The Mark"; and as a painter of heaven- or hell-inflected urban landscapes in the poems "Peter and Mother," which could be an evocation of his childhood in Detroit, and "The Happy Traveler," which reminds me of Rochester, where I spent part of my childhood at the same time as the newly married David and Judith (who was born there) were living a few blocks away. I will conclude with a brief note on poetry, the only one Schubert wrote, which prefaced the selection of his poems in *Five Young American Poets*.

The Mark

Sad as the rain am I now that God has
Graded me with a *B-*; in his class,
I loved the recess, studied the window.
Is it my fault who built me that way? Yet
Even God must suffer at his mistakes.
Why did he lie? Or didn't he know
Who promised me, that of phoenixes, I
Was not to be cremated, but a Glory.

A *B-* hurts; it isn't even
A mediocrity; not an *A* standing there
On its own legs, a smart man; but
A curved Greek, pliant and polite,
Lacking something.

Think of the sinuous bosom
Of a *C*, which sees all, and feigns

Indifference! An open mind is a C, a good
American, friendly, someone you can talk to. A D
On the other hand, stands for
Damn you! Who

Can survive its scurrilous echo?
And E is like an eel, squashy, squishy—
But mud in your eye whichever way you look at it.

As for the sacred excommunication's
F—final is it, finalities
Beyond the grave. And like the question *why,*
Haunting the victim in his tabula rasa.[23]

Peter and Mother

"A hand is writing these lines
On your eyes for journeys
You'll never start for. They're
Transparencies. Wear rubbers
And you will be wise."

In dreams initial A and in the parlor
The chandelier was bright with small toy tears;
At evening the door opened on clematis
And his mother with a shawl ran down the years
To meet someone with an empty lunch-box.
As they returned across the lot—
He listened—in her head was truth
Hansel and Gretel and a bar
Of sweetest song.

> Where the word
> Is shadow of the deed and hard
> Upon it like first crocuses
> In snow . . . "grow up and be
> My tenement house, my brick building!"

This paper representation imperfectly made,
Be like words at a railway station still
Speaking though the train has gone—
The pity strong enough
To tear the four walls down, scatter the children,
The picture of the cow on the wall
Grazing an indifferent pasture.

Talking her trite ghost, the smell
Of lilac is fainter and fainter;
Thinking her worn face is like a face
A whiteness on the brush of some eternal painter.
And always growing farther, trying to hear
Something that was never expressed very
Clearly.

> Her journey ended that was hidden
> In the blindness of his naive skin.[24]

The Happy Traveler

Farewell, O zinnias, tall as teetotalers,
And thou, proud petunias, pastel windows of joy,
Also to you, noble tree trunks, by name
Elm, with your dark bark in the dark rain, couchant

Like comfortable elephants. And you
Mailbox colored robin's egg blue on the poor
House, shy, set back (a poor gentleman but
Irreproachable), with your shutter's robin's egg
Green. You, street, striated with rain like a new penny,
And houses planted by arbor-vitae trees,
By miniature pines that lean against you for
Support—Hail and farewell!

       And I, outside in the rain, look inside
These elms whose branches tip and touch
The slant roof, slain by the four fireplaces
Where life, slowly, life is conventional
In a sheer seersucker dress, with blue eyes,
A red ribbon in her pale hair, eats a sundae,
Glances at the young man.

       O city whose lives
Gather their accumulation of days
Carefully as well-kept lawns.

       Past the proud apartment
Houses, fat as a fat money bag. I wish that I
Might stay in this pleasant, conventional
City, as I study a sturdy clover
Bent back by a dewdrop of rain. But then
From the corner of a mood like Les Sylphides,
Impossible, romantic as certain moons
In certain atmospheres, then you called me
From the corner of the street. And,
Like buttercups, like invitations: I.[25]

A Short Essay on Poetry

A poet who observes his own poetry ends up, in spite of it, by finding nothing to observe, just as a man who pays too much attention to the way he walks, finds his legs walking off from under him. Nevertheless, poets must sometimes look at themselves in order to remember what they are risking. What I see as poetry is a sample of the human scene, its incurably acute melancholia redeemed only by affection. This sample of endurance is innocent and gay: the music of the vowel and consonant is the happy-go-lucky echo of time itself. Without this music there is simply no poem. It borrows further gayety by contrast with the burden it carries—for this exquisite lilt, this dance of sound, must be married to a responsible intelligence before there can occur the poem. Naturally, they are one: meanings and music, metaphor and thought. In the course of poetry's career, perhaps new awarenesses are discovered, really new awarenesses and not verbal combinations brought together in any old way. This rather unimportant novelty is sometimes a play of possibility and sometimes a genuinely new insight: like *Tristram Shandy*, they add something to this Fragment of Life.[26]

Notes ▲ Index

Notes

▲ ▲ ▲ I. JOHN CLARE

1. W. H. Auden, "If I Could Tell You," *Collected Poems,* ed. Edward Mendelson (New York: Random House, 1976), pp. 244–245.
2. Ralph Waldo Emerson, *Emerson in His Journals,* ed. Joel Porter (Cambridge, Mass.: Harvard University Press, 1982), p. 401.
3. George Moore, Introduction to *An Anthology of Pure Poetry* (New York: Liveright, 1973), p. 18.
4. Ibid., pp. 19–20, 32, 37.
5. John Barth, interview, source unidentified; quote revised by Barth in a letter to John Ashbery (electronic mail, April 4, 1999).
6. W. H. Auden, Introduction to *Nineteenth-Century British Minor Poets* (New York: Delacorte, 1966), pp. 15–16.
7. John Clare, "The Autobiography: 1793–1824," *The Prose of John Clare,* ed. J. W. Tibble and Anne Tibble (London: Routledge and Kegan Paul, 1951), p. 88.
8. James Reeves, ed., Introduction to *Selected Poems of John Clare* (London: Heinemann, 1954), pp. xl–xli.
9. John Clare, "To Mary," *John Clare: The Oxford Authors,* ed. Eric Robinson and David Powell (Oxford: Oxford University Press, 1984), p. 342.
10. Donald Davie, "John Clare," *The New Statesman,* LXVII (June 19, 1964), p. 964, in Mark Storey, ed., *Clare: The*

Critical Heritage (London: Routledge and Kegan Paul, 1973),
p. 440.

11. Elaine Feinstein, Introduction to *John Clare: Selected Poems*
(London, 1968), quoted in Storey, Introduction, p. 22.

12. Harold Bloom, "John Clare: The Wordsworthian Shadow,"
*The Visionary Company: A Reading of English Romantic
Poetry,* pp. 450, 451, in Storey, pp. 434, 435.

13. Storey, Introduction, p. 22.

14. Clare, "To Wordsworth," *Selected Poems,* ed. with intro. by
Geoffrey Grigson (Cambridge, Mass.: Harvard University
Press, 1950), p. 178.

15. Clare, "The Elms and the Ashes," in Grigson, p. 233.

16. Clare, "Don Juan A Poem," in *John Clare: Oxford Authors,*
pp. 325, 326.

17. Arthur Symons, Introduction to *Poems by John Clare* (1908),
in Storey, p. 305.

18. Robert Graves, "Peasant Poet," *Hudson Review,* VIII (Spring
1955), pp. 99–105, in Storey, p. 414.

19. Clare, "Journey out of Essex," in *John Clare's Autobiographi-
cal Writings,* ed. Eric Robinson (Oxford: Oxford University
Press, 1983), pp. 158–159.

20. J. Middleton Murry, "Clare and Wordsworth," *The Times
Literary Supplement* (August 21, 1924), p. 511, in Storey,
p. 360.

21. Søren Kierkegaard, *A Kierkegaard Anthology,* ed. Robert
Bretall (Princeton: Princeton University Press, 1973), p. 5.

22. Clare, "I found the poems in the fields," in J. W. Tibble, ed.,
Introduction to *The Poems of John Clare,* 2 vols. (London:
J. M. Dent, 1935), p. viii.

23. Murry, in Storey, p. 362.

24. Clare, "January: A Winters Day," *The Shepherd's Calendar,*
ed. Eric Robinson and Geoffrey Summerfield (London: Oxford
University Press, 1964), p. 3.

25. Clare, "Recollections After an Evening Walk," in *John Clare:
Oxford Authors,* pp. 41–42.

26. Clare, "House or Window Flies," in Reeves, p. 120.

27. Clare, "The Village Minstrel," in Tibble, vol. 1, p. 162.

28. Clare, "The Flitting," in Tibble, vol. 1, p. 251.

29. Clare, "Child Harold," in *John Clare: Oxford Authors,* p. 294.

30. Clare, "I Am," in *John Clare: Oxford Authors,* p. 361.

31. Bloom, in Storey, p. 437.

32. Clare, "A Vision," in *John Clare: Oxford Authors,* p. 343.

33. Edward Thomas, "Women, Nature, and Poetry," *Feminine Influence on the English Poets* (1910), pp. 80–87, in Storey, p. 314.

⋏ ⋏ ⋏ II. THOMAS LOVELL BEDDOES

1. T. S. Eliot, "Whispers of Immortality," *Collected Poems 1909–1962* (New York: Harcourt Brace, 1963), p. 45.

2. Clare, in *John Clare: The Oxford Authors,* ed. Eric Robinson and David Powell (Oxford: Oxford University Press, 1984), pp. 351–352.

3. According to "Cottle, the publisher," quoted by H. W. Donner, Introduction to *Plays and Poems of Thomas Lovell Beddoes,* ed. Donner (Cambridge, Mass.: Harvard University Press, 1950), p. xiv.

4. Sir Humphry Davy, *Fragmentary Remains, Literary and Scientific of Sir Humphry Davy* (London: Churchill, 1858), p. 150; quoted in Donner, Introduction to *Plays and Poems,* pp. xv–xvi.

5. Donner, Introduction to *Plays and Poems,* p. xiv.

6. Ibid.

7. Beddoes, *The Works of Thomas Lovell Beddoes,* ed. H. W. Donner (London: Oxford University Press, 1935), p. 15.

8. John Forster, quoted in Donner, Introduction to *Plays and Poems,* p. xix.

9. George Darley, quoted in Donner, ibid.

10. Beddoes, *Works,* p. 254.

11. H. W. Donner, Introduction, in Beddoes, *Works,* p. xxiii.

12. Walter Savage Landor, quoted in Donner, Introduction to *Plays and Poems,* p. xxxix.

13. Beddoes, *Works,* p. 636.

14. See discussion of the American surgeon Richard Selzer and Beddoes in James R. Thompson, *Thomas Lovell Beddoes,* Twayne English Authors Series (Boston: Twayne, 1985), p. 54.

15. Beddoes, *Works,* p. 487.

16. Ibid., p. 488.

17. See Donner, Introduction to *Plays and Poems,* p. xlv.

18. Beddoes, *Works,* p. 488.

19. Zoë King (Beddoes's cousin), quoted in Edmund Gosse, Introduction to Thomas Lovell Beddoes, *The Poetical Works,* ed. Gosse (London: J. M. Dent, 1890), p. xxxii.

20. Beddoes, *Works,* p. 683.

21. Letter from Robert Browning to Thomas Kelsall, May 22, 1868 (Letter CXI), *The Browning Box: Or, the Life and Works of Thomas Lovell Beddoes,* ed. with intro. by H. W. Donner (London: Routledge and Kegan Paul, 1950), quoted in Judith Higgens, Introduction, *Thomas Lovell Beddoes: Selected Poems,* ed. with intro. by Judith Higgens (Manchester: Fyfield Books/Carcanet Press, 1976), pp. 7, 17 n. 2.

22. Lytton Strachey, "The Last Elizabethan," *Literary Essays* (New York: Harcourt, Brace and World, 1949), pp. 171–172.

23. Gosse, Introduction, in Beddoes, *Poetical Works,* p. xxxvi.

24. Clare, "The Mouse's Nest," in *John Clare: The Oxford Authors,* p. 263.

25. Beddoes, "A Crocodile," *Works,* pp. 237–238.

26. Beddoes, *Works,* from Fragment XXIX, "Death Sweet," p. 243.

27. Beddoes, *Works,* p. 234.

28. From *The Album* (May 1823), quoted in Donner, Introduction to *Plays and Poems,* p. lxxiii.

29. Beddoes, *Works,* p. 283.

30. Thompson, *Thomas Lovell Beddoes,* p. 61.

31. Geoffrey Wagner, "Beddoes, Centennial of a Suicide," *The Golden Horizon* (New York: University Books, 1955), quoted in Thompson, p. 61.

32. Beddoes, *Works,* p. 342.

33. Strachey, "The Last Elizabethan," p. 189.

34. Beddoes, *Works,* p. 255.

35. Beddoes, *Works:* "Fragment of 'Love's Arrow Poisoned,' " p. 254; "Songs from 'The Bride's Tragedy,' " p. 68.

36. Sir Thomas Browne, *Selected Writings,* ed. Sir Geoffrey Keynes (Chicago: University of Chicago Press, 1968), p. 149.

37. Strachey, "The Last Elizabethan," p. 187.

38. George Saintsbury, *A History of English Prosody from the Twelfth Century to the Present Day* (London: Macmillan, 1910), vol. 3, p. 150, quoted by Higgens, *Thomas Lovell Beddoes,* p. 17 n. 1.

39. H. W. Donner, *Thomas Lovell Beddoes: The Making of a Poet* (Oxford: Basil Blackwell, 1935), pp. 277–281.

40. Beddoes, *Works,* pp. 110–111.

▲ ‧ ▲   III. RAYMOND ROUSSEL

1. Michel Butor, "The Methods of Raymond Roussel" (1950), trans. Roderick Masterton, in *Raymond Roussel: Life, Death, and Work: Essays and Stories by Various Hands, Atlas Anthology,* 4 (London: Atlas Press, 1987), pp. 60–71; and Alain Robbe-Grillet, "Riddles and Transparencies in Raymond Roussel" (1963), trans. Barbara Wright, in *Atlas,* 4, pp. 100–105.

2. Here I should say that the day before I delivered this lecture at Harvard, I got a letter from a Rousselian in London telling me that a trunk deposited in a warehouse about 1932, containing a large amount of hitherto unknown Roussel material, had just been found in Paris. Much of this material is now in the Bibliothèque Nationale.

3. Michel Foucault, *Death and the Labyrinth: The World of Raymond Roussel,* trans. Charles Ruas, with introduction by John Ashbery (Garden City, N.Y.: Doubleday, 1986).

4. *Bizarre,* 34–35 (1964), ed. Jean Ferry.

5. John Ashbery, "Re-establishing Raymond Roussel," *Portfolio and Art News Annual,* 6 (Autumn 1962), reprinted in Raymond Roussel, *How I Wrote Certain of My Books,* trans. Trevor Winkfield (New York: Sun, 1977), as "On Raymond Roussel," pp. 43–55; in *How I Wrote Certain of My Books and Other Writings,* ed. Trevor Winkfield (Boston: Exact Change, 1995), as "Introduction"; and in Foucault, as "On Raymond Roussel," with postscript, pp. xiii–xxviii.

6. Rayner Heppenstall, *Raymond Roussel: A Critical Study* (London: Calder and Boyars, 1967); *Impressions of Africa,* trans. Heppenstall and Lindy Foord (Calder and Boyars, 1967).

7. François Caradec, *Vie de Raymond Roussel* (Paris: Pauvert, 1972); see also his *Raymond Roussel* (Paris: Fayard, 1997), a vastly enlarged version incorporating new discoveries.

8. Jean Cocteau, *Opium: Journal d'une désintoxication* (Stock, 1930); trans. E. Boyd (Longmans, 1932; Allen and Unwin, 1933); trans. M. Crosland and S. Road (Owen, 1957; Icon, 1961).

9. Philippe G. Kerbellec, *Comment lire Raymond Roussel* (Paris: Pauvert, 1988); see also his *Raymond Roussel: Au cannibale affable* (Monaco: Rocher, 1994).

10. Caradec, *Vie,* p. xii.

11. Roger Vitrac, "Raymond Roussel" (1928), *Atlas,* 4, p. 53.

12. Roussel, *Comment j'ai écrit certains de mes livres* (Lemerre, 1935), p. 31 (my translation).

13. Ibid., p. 27.

14. Pierre Janet, *De l'Angoisse à l'Extase* (Alcan, 1926), pp. 132–136 (my translation).

15. Cocteau, *Opium,* p. 194.

16. See Ashbery, "Introduction to Documents," in *How I Wrote,* ed. Winkfield (1995), p. 173.

17. Michel Leiris, *Roussel l'ingénu* (Paris: Fata Morgana, 1987), p. 67 (my translation).

18. Ibid., pp. 27–28 (my translation).

19. Vitrac, "Raymond Roussel," p. 50.

20. Roussel, *La Doublure* (Paris: Lemerre, 1897), p. 32 (my translation).

21. Roussel, *La Vue* (Paris: Pauvert, 1963), p. 73 (my translation).

22. Roussel, *Comment j'ai écrit,* p. 30 (my translation).

23. Roussel, *Locus Solus* (Paris: Lemerre, 1914; reprinted, Paris: Pauvert, 1965), p. 191 (my translation).

24. Marcel Duchamp, *Marchand du Sel.*

25. Roussel, *L'Étoile au Front* (Paris: Lemerre, 1925), my translation. For the complete English version, see "The Star on the Forehead," trans. Martin Sorrell, in *Raymond Roussel: Selections from Certain of His Books, Atlas Anthology,* 7 (London: Atlas Press, 1991), pp. 139–226.

26. Robbe-Grillet, "Riddles and Transparencies," in *Atlas,* 4, pp. 105, 100.

27. Leiris, *Roussel l'ingénu,* p. 76.

28. John Cage, "Lecture on Nothing," *Silence: Lectures and Writings* (Middletown, Conn.: Wesleyan University Press, 1961), p. 109.

▲ ▲ ▲   IV. JOHN WHEELWRIGHT

1. Wheelwright's review of *A Joking Word* and *Laura and Francisca* is entitled "Multiplied Bewilderments," *Poetry,* vol. 40 (August 1932), pp. 288–290.

2. Now housed in the Brown University library.

3. Alan M. Wald, *The Revolutionary Imagination: The Poetry and Politics of John Wheelwright and Sherry Mangan* (Chapel Hill: University of North Carolina Press, 1983), pp. 161–162.

4. W. S. Gilbert, "If You're Anxious For to Shine," from *Patience: or Bunthorne's Bride* (1881).

5. Wheelwright, "Bread-Word Giver," *Collected Poems of John Wheelwright*, ed. Alvin H. Rosenfeld (New York: New Directions, 1983), p. 115.

6. Wheelwright, note to "Paul and Virginia," *Collected Poems*, p. 58.

7. Wheelwright, "The Good Boy Who Enjoyed the Cake," *Hound and Horn*, 4 (April–June 1931), p. 428.

8. Wheelwright, note to "Forty Days," *Collected Poems*, p. 57.

9. Wheelwright, note to "Come Over and Help Us," *Collected Poems*, p. 60.

10. Alvin Rosenfeld and S. Foster Damon, "John Wheelwright: New England's Colloquy with the World," *The Southern Review*, VIII, no. 2 (Spring 1972), p. 316.

11. Wheelwright, "Argument," *Mirrors of Venus*, in *Collected Poems*, p. 64.

12. Wheelwright, *Selected Poems*, Poet of the Month (Norfolk, Conn.: New Directions, 1941).

13. Wheelwright, "Verse + Radio = Poetry," in Rosenfeld and Damon, "John Wheelwright," pp. 324–325.

14. Wheelwright, "Back to the Old Farm," Review of *A Further Range* by Robert Frost, *Poetry*, vol. 40 (1936), pp. 45–48.

15. Wheelwright, Review of *U.S. 1* by Muriel Rukeyser, in *Partisan Review*, vol. 4, no. 4 (1938), pp. 54–56.

16. Matthew Josephson, *Life Among the Surrealists* (New York: Holt, Rinehart and Winston, [1962]).

17. Wald, *Revolutionary Imagination*, p. 59.

18. "Phallus," *Collected Poems*, p. 94.

19. "Sophomore," *Collected Poems*, p. 75.

20. "Slow Curtain," *Collected Poems*, p. 10.

21. "Quick Curtain," *Collected Poems*, p. 11.

22. "Why Must You Know?" *Collected Poems*, pp. 23–24.

23. "Any Friend to Any Friend," *Collected Poems*, p. 25.

24. "Death at Leavenworth," *Collected Poems*, p. 66.

25. "Father," *Collected Poems,* p. 78.

26. Wald, *Revolutionary Imagination,* p. 129.

27. Ibid., p. 257 n. 48.

28. "North Atlantic Passage," *Collected Poems,* p. 3.

29. Ibid., p. 6.

30. Ibid., p. 3.

31. Ibid., p. 5.

32. Ibid., pp. 7–8.

33. Quoted in Rosenfeld and Damon, "John Wheelwright," p. 315.

34. Wheelwright, note to "Train Ride," *Collected Poems,* p. 154.

35. "Train Ride," *Collected Poems,* p. 144.

▲ ▲ ▲ V. LAURA RIDING

1. Joyce Piell Wexler, *Laura Riding's Pursuit of Truth* (Athens, Ohio: Ohio University Press, 1979). Since I wrote my lecture much more biographical material has surfaced, notably Deborah Baker's *In Extremis: The Life of Laura Riding* (New York: Grove, 1993), and Richard Perceval Graves, *Robert Graves: The Years with Laura Riding, 1926–1940* (New York: Viking Penguin, 1990). It should be noted that the latter author is Robert Graves's nephew, and hence perhaps not entirely unbiased.

2. Robert Graves, "The Nape of the Neck," *Poems (1914–1926).*

3. Quoted by James Moran, "The Seizin Press of Laura Riding and Robert Graves," *The Black Art* (Summer 1963), p. 35.

4. Wexler, *Riding's Pursuit of Truth,* p. 96.

5. Riding, "Neglected Books," *Antaeus,* 20 (Winter 1976), pp. 155–157. "Rational Meaning" was posthumously published in 1997 by the University Press of Virginia.

6. (Riding) Jackson, *Selected Poems: In Five Sets* (London: Faber, 1970).

7. (Riding) Jackson, *The Telling* (New York: Harper and Row, 1973).

8. Riding and Robert Graves, *A Survey of Modernist Poetry* (London: William Heinemann, 1927; Garden City, N.Y.: Doubleday Doran, 1928; reprinted, St. Clair Shores, Mich.: Scholarly Press, 1972), pp. 11–34.

9. Riding and Robert Graves, *A Pamphlet against Anthologies* (1928; reprinted, New York: AMS, 1970), pp. 96–97, 101.

10. Franz Kafka, *The Diaries of Franz Kafka 1910–1913*, ed. Max Brod, trans. Joseph Kresh (New York: Schocken, 1948), p. 277.

11. Wexler, *Riding's Pursuit of Truth*, p. xii.

12. (Riding) Jackson, *The Poems of Laura Riding: A New Edition of the 1938 Collection* (New York: Persea, 1980), pp. 11, 405.

13. Ibid., pp. 403–404.

14. Wexler, *Riding's Pursuit of Truth*, p. 40.

15. (Riding) Jackson, "Sex, Too," *Experts Are Puzzled* (London: Cape, 1930), p. 24.

16. Riding Gottschalk, *The Close Chaplet* (New York: Adelphi, 1926), pp. 44, 45–46.

17. Ibid., pp. 53–54. A revised, somewhat shorter version can be found in *The Poems of Laura Riding* (1980). Both have their merits, but I prefer the earlier one.

18. Barbara Block Adams, *Enemy Self: Poetry and Criticism of Laura Riding* (Ann Arbor and London: UMI Research Press, 1990), p. 63.

19. Laura Riding, *Collected Poems* (New York: Random House, 1938), pp. 207–208.

20. *First Awakenings: The Early Poems of Laura Riding,* ed. Elizabeth Friedmann, Alan J. Clark, and Robert Nye (Manchester: Carcanet Press, 1992).

21. Quoted in Wexler, *Riding's Pursuit of Truth*, p. 154.

22. Ibid., p. 158.

23. W. H. Auden, *Collected Poems,* ed. Edward Mendelson (New York: Random House, 1976), "Law, say the gardeners, is the

sun": "Law Like Love," p. 208; "This lunar beauty": "This
Lunar Beauty," p. 57; "Jumbled in the common box": "VII.
Domesday Song," in "Ten Songs," p. 213. Mendelson states
in a letter to John Ashbery (electronic mail, May 16, 1999)
that "as it happens, Auden's typescript table of contents for
The Criterion Book of Modern American Verse does survive—
but he typed it after Laura Riding refused permission to use
her poems, so we don't know what WHA wanted to use.
As for the poems that he absorbed early on, it's clear that he
was most affected by the book *Love as Love, Death as Death,*
and the poem he echoed most clearly was 'All Nothing,
Nothing.'"

24. John Ashbery, "The Thinnest Shadow," *Some Trees,* reprinted
    in *The Mooring of Starting Out: The First Five Books of
    Poetry* (Hopewell, N.J.: Ecco, 1997), p. 30.

25. T. S. Matthews, *Jacks and Better* (New York: Harper and Row,
    1977), pp. 321–322.

26. Julian Symons, "An Evening at Maida Vale," *The London
    Magazine* (January 1964), p. 41.

▲   ▲   ▲   VI. DAVID SCHUBERT

 1. John Ashbery, "Schubert's Unfinished," *David Schubert:
    Works and Days, Quarterly Review of Literature Poetry Series
    40th Anniversary Issue,* ed. Theodore Weiss and Renée Weiss
    (Princeton, N.J.: QRL, 1983), p. 308.

 2. William Carlos Williams, letter to Theodore Weiss, July 16,
    1946; reprinted by permission of Theodore Weiss.

 3. Theodore Weiss (1980), in *Works and Days,* p. 232.

 4. W. H. Auden, *Collected Poems* (New York: Random House,
    1976), p. 329.

 5. "No Title," *Works and Days,* p. 65; Frank O'Hara, "For
    David Schubert," *Works and Days,* pp. 299–300.

 6. "A Multi-Auto-Biography," ed. Renée Karol Weiss, *Works and
    Days,* p. 108.

7. Theodore Baird, in "A Multi-Auto-Biography," *Works and Days,* p. 91.
8. "A Multi-Auto-Biography," *Works and Days,* p. 83.
9. *Works and Days,* p. 16.
10. Letter from Judith Schubert to M. D. Zabel, in "A Multi-Auto-Biography," *Works and Days,* p. 272.
11. David Schubert, *Initial A: A Book of Poems* (New York: Macmillan, 1961).
12. Auden, *Collected Poems,* p. 329.
13. Irvin Ehrenpreis, "Homage to Schubert the Poet," *Works and Days,* p. 321.
14. Rachel Hadas, "Eloquence, Inhabited and Uninhabited," *Parnassus* (Fall/Winter 1984), p. 139.
15. *Works and Days,* pp. 3–4.
16. Hadas, "Eloquence," pp. 139, 134.
17. "A Multi-Auto-Biography," *Works and Days,* p. 165.
18. *Works and Days,* p. 312.
19. Hadas, "Eloquence," pp. 138, 136.
20. *Works and Days,* p. 38.
21. Hadas, "Eloquence," p. 144.
22. "A Multi-Auto-Biography," *Works and Days,* pp. 193–194.
23. Schubert, *Works and Days,* p. 20.
24. Ibid., pp. 24–25.
25. Ibid., pp. 35–36.
26. Ibid., p. 1.

Index